I0012550

EXAM AZ-305:

Designing Microsoft Azure Infrastructure Solutions

Complete Exam Preparation

(Latest and Exclusive Practice Tests + Detailed Explanation and References)

Exam AZ-305: Designing Microsoft Azure Infrastructure Solutions New and Exclusive Preparation Book to test your knowledge and help you passing your real AZ-305: Designing Microsoft Azure Infrastructure Solutions Exam on the First Try – Save your time and your money with this new and exclusive Book.

So, if you're looking to test your knowledge, and practice the real exam questions, you are on the right place.

This New Book contains the Latest Questions, Detailed and Exclusive Explanation + References.

Our book covers all topics included in the AZ-305: Designing Microsoft Azure Infrastructure Solutions exam.

This New book is constructed to enhance your confidence to sit for real exam, as you will be testing your knowledge and skills in all the required topics.

To pass the official AZ-305: Designing Microsoft Azure Infrastructure Solutions exam on the first attempt, you need to put in hard work on these AZ-305 questions that provide updated information about the entire exam syllabus.

Welcome!

PRACTICE TEST I

1) You have an Azure subscription that contains a custom application named Application1, developed by Fabrikam, Ltd. Fabrikam developers were assigned RBAC permissions to Application1. All users are licensed for Microsoft 365 E5. You need to recommend a solution to verify whether the Fabrikam developers still require permissions to Application1. The solution must send a monthly email to the manager listing access permissions and automatically revoke unverified permissions. Minimize development effort.

What should you recommend?

A. Create an access review of Application1 in Azure Active Directory (Azure AD).

B. Create an Azure Automation runbook that runs the Get-AzRoleAssignment cmdlet.

C. In Azure AD Privileged Identity Management, create a custom role assignment for Application1.

D. Create an Azure Automation runbook that runs the Get-AzureADUserAppRoleAssignment cmdlet.

2) You have an Azure subscription with a blob container containing multiple blobs. Ten users in the finance department plan to access the blobs during April. You need to recommend a solution for enabling access to the blobs only during April.

What security solution should you include in the recommendation?

A. Shared access signatures (SAS)

B. Conditional Access policies

C. Certificates

D. Access keys

3) You have an Azure AD tenant syncing with an on-premises Active Directory. An internal web app, WebApp1, hosted on-premises, uses Integrated Windows authentication. Some remote users lack VPN access. You need to provide remote users with single sign-on (SSO) access to WebApp1.

Which two features should you include in the solution?

A. Azure AD Application Proxy

B. Azure AD Privileged Identity Management (PIM)

C. Conditional Access policies

D. Azure Arc

E. Azure AD enterprise applications

F. Azure Application Gateway

4) You have an Azure AD tenant (contoso.com) with a security group, Group1, configured for assigned membership. Group1 has 50 members, including 20 guests. You need to recommend a solution for evaluating and managing Group1 membership automatically. What should you include in the recommendation?

A. Implement Azure AD Identity Protection.

B. Change the Membership type of Group1 to Dynamic User.

C. Create an access review.

D. Implement Azure AD Privileged Identity Management (PIM).

5) HOTSPOT:

You are planning to deploy Azure Databricks for a machine learning application.

Data engineers will mount an Azure Data Lake Storage account to the Databricks file system, and permissions to folders are directly granted to the data engineers.

You need to recommend a design for the planned Databrick deployment.

The solution must meet the following requirements:

- **Ensure that the data engineers can only access folders to which they have permissions.**
- **Minimize development effort.**
- **Minimize costs.**

What should you include in the recommendation?

Answer area:

1) Databricks SKU: a. Premium

b. Standard

2) Cluster configuration:

a. Credential passthrough

b. Managed identities

c. MLflow

d. A runtime that contains photon

e. Secret scope

6) HOTSPOT:

You are planning to deploy an Azure web app named App1 that will use Azure Active Directory (Azure AD) authentication.

App1 will be accessed from the internet by users at your company, all of whom have computers running Windows 10 and are joined to Azure AD.

You need to recommend a solution to ensure that users can connect to App1 without being prompted for authentication and can access App1 only from company-owned computers.

Select the appropriate options for each requirement in the answer area.

Answer area:

1) The users can connect to App1 without being prompted for authentication:

a. An Azure AD app registration

b. An Azure AD managed identity

c. Azure AD Application Proxy

2) The user can access App1 only from company-owned computers:

a. An additional Access Policy

b. An Azure AD administrative unit

c. Azure Application Gateway

d. Azure Blueprints

e. Azure Policy

7) *Note: This question is part of a series of questions that present the same scenario. Each question in the series contains a unique solution that might meet the stated goals. Some question sets might have more than one correct solution, while others might not have a correct solution.*

Your company deploys several virtual machines on-premises and to Azure. ExpressRoute is deployed and configured for on-premises to Azure connectivity.

Several virtual machines exhibit network connectivity issues.

You need to analyze the network traffic to identify whether packets are being allowed or denied to the virtual machines.

Solution: Use Azure Traffic Analytics in Azure Network Watcher to analyze the network traffic.

Does this meet the goal?

A. Yes

B. No

8) Your organization deploys numerous virtual machines both on-premises and in Azure, with ExpressRoute facilitating connectivity between on-premises and Azure resources. Some virtual machines are experiencing network connectivity issues.

Your task is to analyze the network traffic to determine

whether packets are being allowed or denied to the virtual machines.

Solution: Utilize Azure Advisor for analyzing the network traffic.

Does this approach align with the goal?

A. Yes

B. No

9) Your company deploys several virtual machines on-premises and to Azure. ExpressRoute is deployed and configured for on-premises to Azure connectivity.

Several virtual machines exhibit network connectivity issues.

You need to analyze the network traffic to identify whether packets are being allowed or denied to the virtual machines.

Solution: Use Azure Network Watcher to run IP flow verify to analyze the network traffic.

Does this meet the goal?

A. Yes

B. No

10) Drag and Drop:

You have an Azure subscription containing Azure virtual machines running Windows Server 2016 and Linux.

You need to use Azure Monitor to design an alerting strategy for security-related events.

Which Azure Monitor Logs tables should you query? To answer, drag the appropriate tables to the correct log types. Each table may be used once, more than once, or not at all.

Select and Place:

Tables:

a. AzureActivity

b. AzureDiagnostics

c. Event

d. Syslog

Answer area:

1. Events from Windows event logs: ....

2. Events from Linux system Logging: ....

11) When designing a large Azure environment with multiple subscriptions and planning to use Azure Policy as part of a governance solution.

To which three scopes can you assign Azure Policy definitions?

A. Azure Active Directory (Azure AD) administrative units

B. Azure Active Directory (Azure AD) tenants

C. subscriptions

D. compute resources

E. resource groups

F. management groups

12) DRAG DROP:

Your on-premises network contains a server named Server1 that runs an ASP.NET application named App1.

You have a hybrid deployment of Azure Active Directory (Azure AD).

You need to recommend a solution to ensure that users sign in by using their Azure AD account and Azure Multi-Factor Authentication (MFA) when they connect to App1 from the internet.

Which three features should you recommend be deployed and configured in sequence? To answer, choose the appropriate features from the list of features to the answer area and arrange them in the correct order.

Select and Place:

Features:

a. A public Azure Load Balancer

b. A managed identity

c. An internal Azure Load Balancer

d. A Conditional Access policy

e. An Azure App Service plan

f. Azure AD Application Proxy

g. An Azure AD enterprise application

Answer area:

1)...

2)...

3)...

13) You are tasked with recommending a solution for generating a monthly report that includes details on all new Azure Resource Manager (ARM) resource deployments within your Azure subscription.

What should be part of your recommendation?

A. Azure Activity Log

B. Azure Advisor

C. Azure Analysis Services

D. Azure Monitor action groups

14) Your company deploys numerous virtual machines both on-premises and in Azure, with ExpressRoute facilitating connectivity between on-premises and Azure. Some virtual machines are experiencing network connectivity problems.

To identify whether packets are being allowed or denied to the virtual machines, you decide to take the following action: Install and configure the Azure Monitoring agent and the Dependency Agent on all the virtual machines, then utilize VM insights in Azure Monitor to analyze the network traffic.

Does this approach achieve the intended goal?

A. Yes

B. No

15) DRAG DROP:

You need to design an architecture to capture the creation of users and the assignment of roles. The captured data must be stored in Azure Cosmos DB.

Which services should you include in the design? To answer, choose the appropriate services to the correct targets. Each service may be used once, more than once, or not at all.

Select and Place:

Azure services:

a. Azure Event Grid

b. Azure Event Hubs

c. Azure Functions

d. Azure Monitor Logs

e. Azure Notifications Hubs

Answer area:

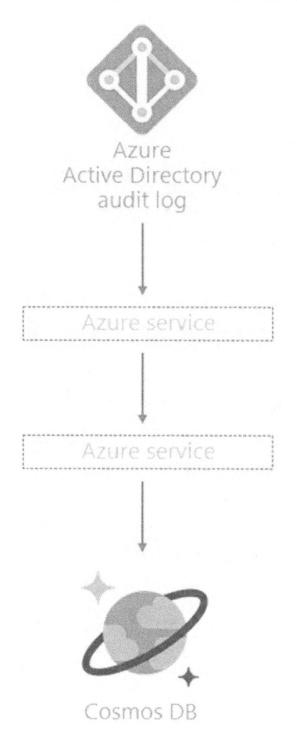

Azure
Active Directory
audit log

Azure service

Azure service

Cosmos DB

16) Your company, named Contoso, Ltd., implements several Azure logic apps that have HTTP triggers. The logic apps provide access to an on-premises web service.

Contoso establishes a partnership with another company named Fabrikam, Inc.

Fabrikam does not have an existing Azure Active Directory (Azure AD) tenant and uses third-party OAuth 2.0 identity management to authenticate its users.

Developers at Fabrikam plan to use a subset of the logic apps to build applications that will integrate with the on-premises web service of Contoso.

You need to design a solution to provide the Fabrikam developers with access to the logic apps. The solution must meet the following requirements:

∞Requests to the logic apps from the developers must be limited to lower rates than the requests from the users at Contoso.

∞ The developers must be able to rely on their existing OAuth 2.0 provider to gain access to the logic apps.

∞ The solution must NOT require changes to the logic apps.

∞ The solution must NOT use Azure AD guest accounts.

What should you include in the solution?

A. Azure Front Door

B. Azure AD Application Proxy

C. Azure AD business-to-business (B2B)

D. Azure API Management

17) You have an Azure subscription with 300 virtual machines running Windows Server 2019.

Your goal is to centrally monitor all warning events in the System logs of these virtual machines.

What should you include in the solution?

Hot area:

Answer area:

1) Resource to create in Azure:

a. An event hub

b. A log analytics workspace

c. A search service

d. A storage account

2) Configuration performance:

a. Create event subscriptions

b. Configure continuous delivery

c. Install the Azure Monitor Agent

d. Modify the membership of the event log readers group.

18) HOTSPOT:

You have several Azure App Service web apps that use Azure Key Vault to store data encryption keys.

Several departments have the following requests to support the web app:

Department	Request
Security	• Review the membership of administrative roles and require users to provide a justification for continued membership. • Get alerts about changes in administrator assignments. • See a history of administrator activation, including which changes administrators made to Azure resources.
Development	• Enable the applications to access Key Vault and retrieve keys for use in code.
Quality Assurance	• Receive temporary administrator access to create and configure additional web apps in the test environment.

Which service should you recommend for each department's request?

To answer, configure the appropriate options in the answer area.

Hot Area:

Answer area:

1) Security:

a. Azure AD Privileged Identity Management.

b. Azure Managed Identity.

c. Azure AD Connect.

d. Azure AD Identity Protection.

2) Development:

a. Azure AD Privileged Identity Management.

b. Azure Managed Identity.

c. Azure AD Connect.

d. Azure AD Identity Protection.

3) Quality Assurance:

a. Azure AD Privileged Identity Management.

b. Azure Managed Identity.

c. Azure AD Connect.

d. Azure AD Identity Protection.

19) HOTSPOT:

Your company has the divisions shown in the following table.

Division	Azure subscription	Azure Active Directory (Azure AD) tenant
East	Sub1, Sub2	East.contoso.com
West	Sub3, Sub4	West.contoso.com

You plan to deploy a custom application to each subscription. The application will contain the following:

∞ A resource group
∞ An Azure web app
∞ Custom role assignments
∞ An Azure Cosmos DB account

You need to use Azure Blueprints to deploy the application to each subscription.
What is the minimum number of objects required to deploy the application?

Hot Area:

Answer area:

1) Management groups:

a. 1

b. 2

c. 3

d. 4

2) Blueprints definitions:

a. 1

b. 2

c. 3

d. 4

3) Blueprints assignments:

a. 1

b. 2

c. 3

d. 4

20) HOTSPOT -

You need to design an Azure policy that will implement the following functionality:

∞ **For new resources, assign tags and values that match the tags and values of the resource group to which the resources are deployed.**

∞ **For existing resources, identify whether the tags and values match the tags and values of the resource group that contains the resources.**

∞ **For any non-compliant resources, trigger auto-generated remediation tasks to create missing tags and values.**

The solution must use the principle of least privilege.

What should you include in the design?

To answer, choose the appropriate options in the answer area.

Hot Area:

Answer area:

1) Azure policy effect to use:

  a. Append

  b. EnforceOPACconstraint

  c. EnforceRegoPolicy

  d. Modify

2) Azure Active Directory (Azure AD) object and role-based access control (RBAC) role to use for the remediation tasks:

a. A managed identity with the Contributor role.

b. A managed identity with the User Access Administrator role.

c. A service principal with the contributor role.

d. A service principal with the User Access Administrator role.

21) HOTSPOT:

You have an Azure subscription that contains the resources shown in the following table.

Name	Type	Account Kind	Location
storage1	Azure Storage account	Storage (general purpose v1)	East US
storage2	Azure Storage account	StorageV2 (general purpose v2)	East US
Workspace1	Azure Log Analytics workspace	**Not applicable**	East US
Workspace2	Azure Log Analytics workspace	**Not applicable**	East US
Hub1	Azure event hub	**Not applicable**	East US

You create an Azure SQL database named DB1 that is hosted in the East US Azure region.

To DB1, you add a diagnostic setting named Settings1. Settings1 archive SQLInsights to storage1 and sends SQLInsights to Workspace1.

For each of the following statements, select Yes if the statement is true. Otherwise, select No.

Hot Area:

Answer area:

1) You can add a new diagnostic setting that archives SQLInsights logs to storage2.

2) You can add a new diagnostic setting that sends SQLInsights logs to workspace2.

3) You can add a new diagnostic setting that sends SQLInsights logs to Hub1.

22) You plan to deploy an Azure SQL database that will store

Personally Identifiable Information (PII).

You need to ensure that only privileged users can view the PII.

What should you include in the solution?

A. dynamic data masking

B. role-based access control (RBAC)

C. Data Discovery & Classification

D. Transparent Data Encryption (TDE)

23) You plan to deploy an app that will use an Azure Storage account.

You need to deploy the storage account. The storage account must meet the following requirements:

- Store the data for multiple users.
- Encrypt each user's data by using a separate key.
- Encrypt all the data in the storage account by using customer-managed keys.

What should you deploy?

A. files in a premium file share storage account

B. blobs in a general purpose v2 storage account

C. blobs in an Azure Data Lake Storage Gen2 account

D. files in a general purpose v2 storage account

24) HOTSPOT -

You have an Azure App Service web app that uses a system-assigned managed identity.

You need to recommend a solution to store the settings of the web app as secrets in an Azure key vault. The solution must meet the following requirements:

- Minimize changes to the app code.
- Use the principle of least privilege.

What should you include in the recommendation?

To answer, choose the appropriate options in the answer area.

Hot Area:

Answer area:

1) Key vault integration method:

a. Key vault references in application settings

b. Key vault references in Appsettings.json

c. Key vault references in Web.config

d. Key vault SDK

2) Key vault permissions for the managed identity:

a. Keys: Gey

b. keys: List and Get

c. Secrets: Get

d. Secrets: List and Get

25) You plan to deploy an application named App1 that will run on five Azure virtual machines. Additional virtual machines will be deployed later to run App1.

You need to recommend a solution to meet the following requirements for the virtual machines that will run App1:

- Ensure that the virtual machines can authenticate to

Azure Active Directory (Azure AD) to gain access to an Azure key vault, Azure Logic Apps instances, and an Azure SQL database.

- Avoid assigning new roles and permissions for Azure services when you deploy additional virtual machines.
- Avoid storing secrets and certificates on the virtual machines.
- Minimize administrative effort for managing identities.

Which type of identity should you include in the recommendation?

A. a system-assigned managed identity

B. a service principal that is configured to use a certificate

C. a service principal that is configured to use a client secret

D. a user-assigned managed identity

26) You have the resources shown in the following table:

Name	Type
AS1	Azure Synapse Analytics instance
CDB1	Azure Cosmos DB SQL API account

CDB1 hosts a container that stores continuously updated operational data.

You are designing a solution that will use AS1 to analyze the operational data daily.

You need to recommend a solution to analyze the data without affecting the performance of the operational data store.

What should you include in the recommendation?

A. Azure Cosmos DB change feed

B. Azure Data Factory with Azure Cosmos DB and Azure Synapse Analytics connectors

C. Azure Synapse Link for Azure Cosmos DB

D. Azure Synapse Analytics with PolyBase data loading

27) HOTSPOT:

You deploy several Azure SQL Database instances.

You plan to configure the Diagnostics settings on the databases as shown in the following exhibit.

Diagnostics setting

💾 Save   ✕ Discard   🗑 Delete   ☺ Provide feedback

A diagnostic setting specifies a list of categories of platform logs and/or metrics that you want to collect from a resource and one or more destinations that you would stream them to. Normal usage charges for the destination will occur. Learn more about the different log

categories and contents of those logs

Diagnostic setting name   Diagnostic1

Category details

log

	Retention (days)
☑ SQLInsights	90 ✓
☑ AutomaticTuning	30 ✓
☐ QueryStoreRuntimeStatistics	0
☐ QueryStoreWaitStatistics	0
☐ Errors	0
☐ DatabaseWaitStatistics	0
☐ Timeouts	0
☐ Blocks	0
☐ Deadlocks	0

metric

	Retention (days)
☐ Basic	0

Destination details

☑ Send to Log Analytics

Subscription

| Azure Pass - Sponsorship | ⌄ |

Log Analytics workspace

| sk200814 (eastus) | ⌄ |

☑ Archive to a storage account

   ⓘ Showing all storage accounts including classic storage accounts

Location
East US

Subscription

| Azure Pass - Sponsorship | ⌄ |

Storage account *

| contoso20 | ⌄ |

☐ Stream to an event hub

Choose the answer choice that completes each statement based on the information presented in the graphic.

Hot Area:

Answer area:

1) The amount of time that SQLInsights data will be stored in blob storage is [answer choice]

a. 30 days

b. 90 days

c. 730 days

d. indefinite

2) The maximum amount of time that SQLInsights data can be stored in Azure Log Analytics is [answer choice]

a. 30 days

b. 90 days

c. 730 days

d. indefinite

28) For an application with 6,000 users handling vacation requests that currently manages its own credentials and doesn't support identity providers, you intend to upgrade it to use single sign-on (SSO) authentication through an Azure Active Directory (Azure AD) application registration.

What SSO method should be employed?

A. Utilize header-based SSO.

B. Implement SAML-based SSO.

C. Employ password-based SSO.

D. Integrate OpenID Connect for SSO.

29) HOTSPOT -

You have an Azure subscription that contains a virtual network named VNET1 and 10 virtual machines. The virtual machines are connected to VNET1.

You need to design a solution to manage the virtual machines from the internet. The solution must meet the following

requirements:

∞ **Incoming connections to the virtual machines must be authenticated by using Azure Multi-Factor Authentication (MFA) before network connectivity is allowed.**

∞ **Incoming connections must use TLS and connect to TCP port 443.**

∞ **The solution must support RDP and SSH.**

What should you include in the solution?

To answer, choose the appropriate options in the answer area.

Hot Area:

Answer area:

1) The provide access to virtual machines on VNET1, use:

a. Azure Bastion

b. Just-in-time (JIT) VM access

c. Azure Web Application Firewall (WAF) in Azure Front Door

2) To enforce Azure MFA, use:

a. An Azure Identity Governance access package

b. A Conditional access policy that has the cloud apps assignment set to Azure Windows VM sign-in

c. A Conditional access policy that has the cloud apps assignment set to Microsoft Azure Management

30) In the process of designing an Azure governance solution, where it's essential to easily identify Azure resources based on operational information such as environment, owner, department, and cost center

You need to ensure that you can use the operational information when you generate reports for the Azure resources.

What should you include in the solution?

A. Implement an Azure data catalog utilizing the Azure REST API as a data source.

B. Establish an Azure management group with parent groups to create a hierarchy.

C. Enforce tagging rules using an Azure policy.

D. Utilize Azure Active Directory (Azure AD) administrative units.

31) A company named Contoso, Ltd. has an Azure Active Directory (Azure AD) tenant that is integrated with Microsoft 365 and an Azure subscription.

Contoso has an on-premises identity infrastructure. The infrastructure includes servers that run Active Directory Domain Services (AD DS) and Azure AD Connect.

Contoso has a partnership with a company named Fabrikam. Inc. Fabrikam has an Active Directory forest and a Microsoft 365 tenant. Fabrikam has the same on- premises identity infrastructure components as Contoso.

A team of 10 developers from Fabrikam will work on an Azure solution that will be hosted in the Azure subscription of Contoso. The developers must be added to the Contributor role for a resource group in the Contoso subscription.

You need to recommend a solution to ensure that Contoso can assign the role to the 10 Fabrikam developers. The solution must ensure that the Fabrikam developers use their existing

credentials to access resources

What should you recommend?

A. In the Azure AD tenant of Contoso. create cloud-only user accounts for the Fabrikam developers.

B. Configure a forest trust between the on-premises Active Directory forests of Contoso and Fabrikam.

C. Configure an organization relationship between the Microsoft 365 tenants of Fabrikam and Contoso.

D. In the Azure AD tenant of Contoso, create guest accounts for the Fabnkam developers.

32) Your company has the divisions shown in the following table.

Division	Azure subscription	Azure Active Directory (Azure AD) tenant
East	Sub1	Contoso.com
West	Sub2	Fabrikam.com

Sub1 contains an Azure App Service web app named App1. App1 uses Azure AD for single-tenant user authentication. Users from contoso.com can authenticate to App1.
You need to recommend a solution to enable users in the fabrikam.com tenant to authenticate to App1.

What should you recommend?

A. Configure the Azure AD provisioning service.

B. Enable Azure AD pass-through authentication and update the sign-in endpoint.

C. Use Azure AD entitlement management to govern external users.

D. Configure Azure AD join.

33) HOTSPOT -

Your company has 20 web APIs that were developed in-house.

The company is developing 10 web apps that will use the web APIs. The web apps and the APIs are registered in the company s Azure Active Directory (Azure

AD) tenant. The web APIs are published by using Azure API Management.

You need to recommend a solution to block unauthorized requests originating from the web apps from reaching the web APIs. The solution must meet the following requirements:

∞ Use Azure AD-generated claims.

Minimize configuration and management effort.

What should you include in the recommendation?

To answer, choose the appropriate options in the answer area.

Hot Area:

Answer area:

1) Grant permissions to allow the web apps access the web APIs by using:

 a. Azure AD

b. Azure API Management

 c. The web APIs

2) Configure a JSON Web Token (JWT) validation policy by using:

a. Azure AD

b. Azure API Management

c. The web APIs

34) To generate a monthly report of all new Azure Resource Manager (ARM) resource deployments in your Azure subscription, what recommendation should you provide?

A. Implement Azure Log Analytics.

B. Utilize Azure Arc.

C. Implement Azure Analysis Services.

D. Use Application Insights.

35) You have an Azure subscription that contains 1,000 resources.

You need to generate compliance reports for the subscription. The solution must ensure that the resources can be grouped by department.

What should you use to organize the resources?

A. application groups and quotas

B. Azure Policy and tags

C. administrative units and Azure Lighthouse

D. resource groups and role assignments

36) While developing an app that reads activity logs for an Azure subscription using Azure Functions, and aiming to minimize administrative effort for authentication.

You need to recommend an authentication solution for Azure Functions.

what recommendation should be included?

A. Create an enterprise application in Azure AD

B. Set up a system-assigned managed identities

C. Utilize shared access signatures (SAS)

D. An Application registration in Azure AD

37) You have an Azure AD tenant named contoso.com that has a security group named Group1. Group1 is configured for assigned memberships. Group1 has 50 members, including 20 guest users.

You need to recommend a solution for evaluating the membership of Group1. The solution must meet the following requirements:

• The evaluation must be repeated automatically every three months.

• Every member must be able to report whether they need to be in Group1.

• Users who report that they do not need to be in Group1 must be removed from Group1 automatically.

• Users who do not report whether they need to be in Group1 must be removed from Group1 automatically.

What should you include in the recommendation?

A. Implement Azure AD Identity Protection.

B. Change the Membership type of Group1 to Dynamic User.

C. Create an access review.

D. Implement Azure AD Privileged Identity Management (PIM).

38) HOTSPOT:

You have an Azure subscription named Sub1 that is linked to an Azure AD tenant named contoso.com.

You plan to implement two ASP.NET Core apps named App1 and App2 that will be deployed to 100 virtual machines in Sub1. Users will sign in to App1 and App2 by using their contoso.com credentials.

App1 requires read permissions to access the calendar of the signed-in user. App2 requires write permissions to access the calendar of the signed-in user.

You need to recommend an authentication and authorization solution for the apps. The solution must meet the following requirements:

· Use the principle of least privilege.

· Minimize administrative effort.

What should you include in the recommendation? To answer, choose the appropriate options in the answer area.

Answer area:

1) Authentication:

a. Application registration in Azure AD

b. A system-assigned managed identity

c. A user-assigned managed identity

2) Authorization:

a. Application permissions

b. Azure role-based access control (Azure RBAC)

c. Delegated permissions

39) HOTSPOT:

You have an Azure AD tenant that contains a management group named MG1.
You have the Azure subscriptions shown in the following table.

Name	Management group
Sub1	MG1
Sub2	MG2
Sub3	Tenant Root Group

The subscriptions contain the resource groups shown in the following table.

Name	Subscription
RG1	Sub1
RG2	Sub2
RG3	Sub3

The subscription contains the Azure AD security groups shown in the following table.

Name	Member of
Group1	Group3
Group2	Group3
Group3	*None*

The subscription contains the user accounts shown in the following table.

Name	Member of
User1	Group1
User2	Group2
User3	Group1, Group2

You perform the following actions:

Assign User3 the Contributor role for Sub1.
Assign Group1 the Virtual Machine Contributor role for MG1.

Assign Group3 the Contributor role for the Tenant Root Group.

For each of the following statements, choose Yes if the statement is true. Otherwise, select No.

Answer area:

Statements:

1) User1 can create a new virtual machine in RG1

2) User2 can grant permissions to Group2

3) User3 can create a storage account in RG2

40) HOTSPOT:

You have an Azure subscription that contains an Azure key vault named KV1 and a virtual machine named VM1. VM1 runs Windows Server 2022: Azure Edition.

You plan to deploy an ASP.Net Core-based application named App1 to VM1.

You need to configure App1 to use a system-assigned managed identity to retrieve secrets from KV1. The solution must minimize development effort.

What should you do?

To answer, choose the appropriate options in the answer area.

Answer area:

1) Configure App1 to use OAuth 2.0:

a. Authorization code grant flows

b. Client credentials grant flows

c. Implicit grant flows

2) Configure App1 to use REST API call to retrieve an authentication token from the:

a. Aure Instance Metadata Service (MDS) endpoint

b. OAuth 2.0 access token endpoint of Azure AD

C. OAuth 2.0 access token endpoint of Microsoft Identity Platform

41) To recommend a solution for generating a monthly report of all new Azure Resource Manager (ARM) resource deployments in your Azure subscription, what should be

included?

A. Implement Azure Arc.

B. Utilize Azure Monitor metrics.

C. Leverage Azure Advisor.

D. Set up Azure Log Analytics.

42) DRAG DROP:

You have an Azure AD tenant that contains an administrative unit named MarketingAU. MarketingAU contains 100 users.

You create two users named User1 and User2.

You need to ensure that the users can perform the following actions in MarketingAU:

· User1 must be able to create user accounts.

· User2 must be able to reset user passwords.

Which role should you assign to each user? To answer, drag the appropriate roles to the correct users.

Each role may be used once, more than once, or not at all.

Roles:

a. Helpdesk Administrator for MarketingAU

b. Helpdesk Administrator for the tenant

c. User Administrator for MarketingAU

d. User Administrator for the tenant

Answer Area:

1) User1:...

2) User2:...

43) HOTSPOT:

You are designing an app that will be hosted on Azure virtual machines that run Ubuntu. The app will use a third-party email service to send email messages to users. The third-party email service requires that the app authenticate by using an API key.

You need to recommend an Azure Key Vault solution for storing and accessing the API key.

The solution must minimize administrative effort.

What should you recommend using to store and access the key?

To answer, choose the appropriate options in the answer area.

Answer area:

1) Storage:

a. Certificate

b. Key

c. Secret

2) Access:

a. An API token

b. A managed service identity (MSI)

c. A service principal

44) DRAG DROP:

You have two app registrations named App1 and App2 in Azure AD. App1 supports role-based access control (RBAC) and includes a role named Writer.

You need to ensure that when App2 authenticates to access App1, the tokens issued by Azure AD include the Writer role claim.

Which blade should you use to modify each app registration?

To answer, choose the appropriate blades to the correct app registrations. Each blade may be used once, more than once, or not at all.

Blades:

a. API permissions

b. App roles

c. Token configuration

Answer area:

1) App1: ....

2) App2: ....

45) You have an Azure subscription.

You plan to deploy a monitoring solution that will include the following:

• Azure Monitor Network Insights

• Application Insights

• Microsoft Sentinel

• VM insights

The monitoring solution will be managed by a single team.

What is the minimum number of Azure Monitor workspaces required?

A. 1

B. 2

C. 3

D. 4

46) HOTSPOT:

Case Study:

In this examination, case studies are not individually timed, and candidates have the flexibility to allocate as much time as needed for each case. However, it's essential to be mindful that there might be multiple case studies and sections in the exam. To successfully complete all the questions within the provided time, candidates must effectively manage their time.

To respond to the inquiries presented in a case study, it is necessary to consult the information provided within the case study. Case studies may include exhibits and additional resources offering more insights into the described scenario. Each question stands alone and is not dependent on other questions within the case study.

Overview:

Fabrikam, Inc. is an engineering company that has offices throughout Europe. The company has a main office in London and three branch offices in Amsterdam, Berlin, and Rome.

Existing Environment: Active Directory Environment

The network contains two Active Directory forests named corp.fabrikam.com and rd.fabrikam.com. There are no trust relationships between the forests.

Corp.fabrikam.com is a production forest that contains identities used for internal user and computer authentication.

Rd.fabrikam.com is used by the research and development (R&D) department only. The R&D department is restricted to using on-premises resources only.

Existing Environment: Network Infrastructure

Each office contains at least one domain controller from the corp.fabrikam.com domain. The main office contains all the domain controllers for the rd.fabrikam.com forest.

All the offices have a high-speed connection to the internet.

An existing application named WebApp1 is hosted in the data center of the London office. WebApp1 is used by customers to place and track orders. WebApp1 has a web tier that uses Microsoft Internet Information Services (IIS) and a database tier that runs Microsoft SQL Server 2016. The web tier and the database tier are deployed to virtual machines that run on Hyper-V.

The IT department currently uses a separate Hyper-V environment to test updates to WebApp1.

Fabrikam purchases all Microsoft licenses through a Microsoft Enterprise Agreement that includes Software Assurance.

Existing Environment: Problem Statements

The use of WebApp1 is unpredictable. At peak times, users often report delays. At other times, many resources for WebApp1 are underutilized.

Requirements: Planned Changes

Fabrikam plans to move most of its production workloads to Azure during the next few years, including virtual machines that rely on Active Directory for authentication.

As one of its first projects, the company plans to establish a hybrid identity model, facilitating an upcoming Microsoft 365 deployment.

All R&D operations will remain on-premises.

Fabrikam plans to migrate the production and test instances of WebApp1 to Azure.

Requirements: Technical Requirements

Fabrikam identifies the following technical requirements:

· Website content must be easily updated from a single point.

· User input must be minimized when provisioning new web app instances.

· Whenever possible, existing on-premises licenses must be used to reduce cost.

· Users must always authenticate by using their corp.fabrikam.com UPN identity.

· Any new deployments to Azure must be redundant in case an Azure region fails.

· Whenever possible, solutions must be deployed to Azure by using the Standard pricing tier of Azure App Service.

· An email distribution group named IT Support must be notified of any issues relating to the directory synchronization services.

· In the event that a link fails between Azure and the on-premises network, ensure that the virtual machines hosted in Azure can authenticate to Active Directory.

• Directory synchronization between Azure Active Directory (Azure AD) and corp.fabrikam.com must not be affected by a link failure between Azure and the on-premises network.

Requirements: Database Requirements

Fabrikam identifies the following database requirements:

• Database metrics for the production instance of WebApp1 must be available for analysis so that database administrators can optimize the performance settings.

• To avoid disrupting customer access, database downtime must be minimized when databases are migrated.

• Database backups must be retained for a minimum of seven years to meet compliance requirements.

Requirements: Security Requirements

Fabrikam identifies the following security requirements:

• Company information including policies, templates, and data must be inaccessible to anyone outside the company.

• Users on the on-premises network must be able to authenticate to corp.fabrikam.com if an internet link fails.

• Administrators must be able authenticate to the Azure portal by using their corp.fabrikam.com credentials.

• All administrative access to the Azure portal must be secured by using multi-factor authentication (MFA).

• The testing of WebApp1 updates must not be visible to anyone outside the company.

To meet the authentication requirements of Fabrikam, what should you include in the solution?

To answer, choose the appropriate options in the answer area.

Answer area:

1) Minimum number of Azure AD tenants:

a. 0

b. 1

c. 2

d. 3

e. 4

2) Minimum number of conditional access policies to create:

a. 0

b. 1

c. 2

d. 3

e. 4

47) Within your Azure subscription, there are 10 web apps integrated with Azure Active Directory (Azure AD), and these applications are utilized by users associated with diverse project teams.

The users frequently move between projects.

You are tasked with proposing an access management solution for the web apps, and this solution must satisfy the following requirements:

• The users must only have access to the app of the project to which they are assigned currently.

• Project managers must verify which users have access to their project's app and remove users that are no longer assigned to their project.

• Once every 30 days, the project managers must be prompted automatically to verify which users are assigned to their projects.

What should you include in the recommendation?

A. Azure AD Identity Protection

B. Microsoft Defender for Identity

C. Microsoft Entra Permissions Management

D. Microsoft Entra ID Governance

48) Hotspot:

You have an Azure subscription with 50 Azure SQL databases. You've crafted an Azure Resource Manager (ARM) template called Template1 to activate Transparent Data Encryption (TDE).

Your objective is to establish an Azure Policy definition named Policy1, utilizing Template1, to enforce TDE for any Azure SQL databases found to be noncompliant.

Configure Policy1 by selecting the appropriate options in the answer area.

Answer area:

1) Set available effects to:

a. DeploylfNotExists

b. EnforceRegoPolicy

c. Modify

2) Include in the definition:

a. The identity required to perform the remediation task

b. The scopes of the policy assignments

c. The role-based access control (RBAC) roles required to perform the remediation task

49) You have an Azure subscription containing a tiered application named App1, distributed across multiple containers hosted in Azure Container Instances. Your goal is to implement an Azure Monitor monitoring solution for App1 with the following requirements:

Support synthetic transaction monitoring to monitor traffic between App1 components.

Minimize development effort.

What components should you incorporate into the solution?

A. Network insights

B. Application Insights

C. Container insights

D. Log Analytics Workspace insights

50) HOTSPOT:

You have an Azure subscription that contains the resources shown in the following table:

Name	Type	Description
App1	Azure App Service app	None
Workspace1	Log Analytics workspace	Configured to use a pay-as-you-go pricing tier
App1Logs	Log Analytics table	Hosted in Workspace1 Configured to use the Analytics Logs data plan

Log files from App1 are registered to App1Logs. An average of 120 GB of log data is ingested per day.

You configure an Azure Monitor alert that will be triggered if the App1 logs contain error messages.

You need to minimize the Log Analytics costs associated with App1. The solution must meet the following requirements:

• Ensure that all the log files from App1 are ingested to App1Logs.

• Minimize the impact on the Azure Monitor alert.

Which resource should you modify, and which modification should you perform?

To answer, choose the appropriate options in the answer area.

Answer area:

1) Resource:

  a. App1

  b. App1Logs

  c. Workspace1

2) Modification:

a. Change to a commitment pricing tier

b. Change to the Basic Logs data plan

c. Set a daily cap

ANSWERS AND EXPLANATION

1) A

For the given scenario, the recommended solution is:

A. Create an access review of Application1 in Azure Active Directory (Azure AD).

Explanation:

Access reviews in Azure AD allow you to efficiently manage group memberships, access permissions, and roles.

By creating an access review for Application1, you can periodically review and verify the RBAC permissions assigned to Fabrikam developers.

Access reviews can be configured to send email notifications to designated reviewers, in this case, the manager of the developers, listing the access permissions.

If the manager does not verify an access permission during the review, the solution can automatically revoke that permission.

Access reviews are designed for managing and validating access efficiently, minimizing development effort.

Option B and D involve creating Azure Automation runbooks, which might require more development effort and are not specifically designed for access reviews. Option C, Azure AD Privileged Identity Management, is more suitable for managing just-in-time privileged access rather than periodic reviews of application-specific permissions.

Reference:

https://learn.microsoft.com/en-us/azure/active-directory/governance/access-reviews-overview

Access reviews in Azure Active Directory (Azure AD), part of Microsoft Entra, enable organizations to efficiently manage group memberships, access to enterprise applications, and role assignments. User's access can be reviewed regularly to make sure only the right people have continued access.

2) A

The recommended solution for enabling access to the blobs' only during April is:

A. Shared access signatures (SAS)

Explanation:

Shared Access Signatures (SAS) provide a way to grant limited access to resources in Azure, including blobs in a storage account.

You can create a SAS token with specific permissions (read, write, delete, etc.) and set an expiration date.

By generating SAS tokens with an expiration date set to the end of April, you can control access to the blobs for the specified time period.

Conditional Access policies (Option B) are more focused on controlling access based on conditions like user identity, device, and location but may not provide fine-grained control over time-based access.

Certificates (Option C) and Access keys (Option D) are more related to authentication mechanisms rather than time-based access control.

To enable access to blobs in a container during the month of April only, use shared access signatures (SAS). SAS tokens can be generated with an expiration time and can be scoped to provide granular access control. SAS tokens can easily be generated and distributed to the ten finance department users who need access to the blobs during the month of April. SAS tokens will no longer be valid once they expire, fulfilling the requirement to restrict access to the blobs during the month of April only. Conditional Access policies and certificates/access keys are not suitable for this task.

Reference:

https://learn.microsoft.com/en-us/azure/storage/common/authorize-data-access#understand-authorization-for-data-operations

Shared access signatures for blobs, files, queues, and tables. Shared access signatures (SAS) provide limited delegated access to resources in a storage account via a signed URL. The signed URL specifies the permissions granted to the resource and the interval over which the signature is valid. A service SAS or account SAS is signed with the account key, while the user delegation SAS is signed with Azure AD credentials and applies to blobs only.

3) AE

To provide remote users with single sign-on (SSO) access to WebApp1 when the Azure AD tenant is syncing with an on-premises Active Directory, you should include the following two features in the solution:

A. Azure AD Application Proxy

Explanation: Azure AD Application Proxy allows you to securely publish on-premises applications, such as WebApp1, for remote access. It provides SSO capabilities, even for users without VPN access.

E. Azure AD Enterprise Applications

Explanation: Azure AD Enterprise Applications allow you to integrate and manage external applications in Azure AD. You can configure the necessary settings for WebApp1 to enable SSO and seamless authentication for remote users.

Options B, C, D, and F are not directly related to providing remote SSO access to on-premises applications using Integrated Windows authentication.

Azure App proxy for connecting without vpn and Enterprise App for SSO

It's required to download connector under (Application Proxy) and create a new application under (Enterprise Application), however for (Pre-Authentication) option, you can choose "Passthrough" or "Azure Active Directory", and both will work, but it's recommended to use "Azure Active Directory" so you can take advantage of using conditional access and MFA. Answer is (A) & (E) as they're both required as part of the solution to work, whereas (C) is just an optional feature.

Reference:

https://docs.microsoft.com/en-us/azure/active-directory/app-proxy/application-proxy-add-on-premises-application

4) C

- An access review is an Azure AD feature that enables administrators to review group memberships and application assignments, and allows group members to confirm whether they still require access. This enables every member to report whether they need to be in Group1, and if they do not, the access review can be configured to remove them automatically.

- An access review can be set up to repeat automatically every three months, as required by the scenario.

- Changing the Membership type of Group1 to Dynamic User is not a suitable solution for evaluating the membership of a security group with assigned membership. Dynamic user groups are based on rules and criteria, and do not include manually assigned members.

- Implementing Azure AD Identity Protection is not relevant to evaluating the membership of a security group.

- Implementing Azure AD Privileged Identity Management (PIM) is used for managing access to privileged roles in Azure AD, and is not relevant to the scenario.

Azure Active Directory (Azure AD) access reviews enable organizations to efficiently manage group memberships, access to enterprise applications, and role assignments. User's access can be reviewed on a regular basis to make sure only the right people have continued access.

Reference:

https://docs.microsoft.com/en-us/azure/active-directory/governance/access-reviews-overview

5) 1. a, 2. a

Recommended design for the planned Databricks deployment that meets the given requirements:

- Databricks SKU: Premium

- Premium SKU provides access control for DBFS root and FUSE mount points. This will ensure that the data engineers can only access folders to which they have permissions.

- Cluster Configuration: Credentials passthrough

- Credentials passthrough allows users to authenticate with Azure Data Lake Storage using their own Azure AD credentials. This minimizes development effort and costs, as it does not require additional Azure AD application registration and service principal management.

Therefore, the recommended design for the planned Databricks deployment is to use Premium SKU for access control of DBFS root and FUSE mount points, and to configure credentials passthrough for authentication with Azure Data Lake Storage. This design meets the requirements of ensuring data engineers can only access folders to which they have permissions, minimizing development effort and costs.

Databricks SKU should be a Premium plan. As the doc states both cloud storage access and credential passthrough features will need a Premium plan.

https://docs.microsoft.com/en-us/azure/databricks/sql/user/

security/cloud-storage-access

https://docs.microsoft.com/en-us/azure/databricks/security/
credential-passthrough/adls-passthrough#adls-aad-credentials

6)

1: a. Azure AD app registration

- Azure AD app registration is essential to integrate the web application (App1) with Azure AD.

By doing this, you can leverage Azure AD's authentication mechanisms, including SSO. Once App1 is registered in Azure AD and configured for SSO, users who are already signed in to their Azure AD account can access the application without being prompted for authentication again.

https://learn.microsoft.com/en-us/azure/active-directory/
develop/app-objects-and-service-principals?tabs=browser

2: a. Conditional Access policy

- Azure AD Conditional Access policies allow you to define and enforce specific conditions under which users can access applications.

In this scenario, you can create a Conditional Access policy that specifies that App1 can only be accessed from devices that are Azure.

Reference:

https://learn.microsoft.com/en-us/azure/active-directory/
conditional-access/overview

https://docs.microsoft.com/en-us/azure/active-directory/

manage-apps/what-is-application-management

7) B

(Traffic Analytics) under (Network Watcher) gives you statistical data and traffic visualization like total inbound and outbound flows and the number of deployed NSGs. However, it doesn't give you information if packets are allowing of denied. Check screenshot in the following reference: https://docs.microsoft.com/en-us/azure/network-watcher/traffic-analytics

(IP Flow Verify) under (Network Watcher) gives you option to verify if traffic is allowed or denied.

Extra explanation:

Azure Traffic Analytics in Azure Network Watcher is designed to analyze traffic between Azure virtual machines. It does not provide visibility into on-premises virtual machines connected via ExpressRoute. Since the scenario mentions network connectivity issues with several virtual machines, including on-premises ones, using Azure Traffic Analytics alone won't provide the comprehensive analysis needed for both on-premises and Azure-connected virtual machines.

For a comprehensive analysis of network traffic between on-premises and Azure, you might consider using a network monitoring solution that can capture and analyze traffic on both sides of the ExpressRoute connection. Third-party network monitoring tools or Azure Monitor with Log Analytics could be considered for this purpose.

Check screenshot in the following reference: https://docs.microsoft.com/en-us/azure/network-watcher/network-watcher-ip-flow-verify-overview

8) B

Azure Advisor is a service that provides best practices and recommendations for improving the performance, security, and reliability of your Azure resources. However, it does not offer specific capabilities for analyzing network traffic or identifying whether packets are being allowed or denied.

To troubleshoot network connectivity issues and analyze network traffic in the scenario described, you should consider using tools like Azure Network Watcher. Network Watcher includes features such as Connection Monitor, IP Flow Verify, and Traffic Analytics, which are designed for network diagnostics and troubleshooting in Azure environments. Alternatively, third-party network monitoring solutions may also be considered for a more comprehensive analysis, especially when dealing with both on-premises and Azure-connected virtual machines.

Will require IP flow verify.

Reference:

https://learn.microsoft.com/en-us/azure/network-watcher/network-watcher-ip-flow-verify-overview

IP flow verify checks if a packet is allowed or denied to or from a virtual machine. The information consists of direction, protocol, local IP, remote IP, local port, and a remote port. If the packet is denied by a security group, the name of the rule that denied the packet is returned. While any source or destination IP can be chosen, IP flow verify helps administrators quickly diagnose connectivity issues from or to the internet and from or to the on-premises environment.

9) A

IP flow verify checks if a packet is allowed or denied to or from a virtual machine.

Using Azure Network Watcher to run IP flow verify is a suitable solution for analyzing network traffic and determining whether packets are being allowed or denied to the virtual machines. IP flow verify allows you to check if traffic is allowed or denied between specified source and destination IP addresses.

So, in this case, the solution meets the goal of analyzing network traffic to identify whether packets are being allowed or denied to the virtual machines.

Reference:

https://learn.microsoft.com/en-us/azure/network-watcher/network-watcher-ip-flow-verify-overview

IP flow verify checks if a packet is allowed or denied to or from a virtual machine. The information consists of direction, protocol, local IP, remote IP, local port, and a remote port. If the packet is denied by a security group, the name of the rule that denied the packet is returned. While any source or destination IP can be chosen, IP flow verify helps administrators quickly diagnose connectivity issues from or to the internet and from or to the on-premises environment.

10)

1) Windows: c. Event.

2) Linux: d. Syslog

To design an alerting strategy for security-related events in

Azure Monitor, you should query the following Azure Monitor Logs tables:

1. Event - This table contains security events and other system events that are generated by Windows operating systems. The table includes information about the event, such as the event ID, event source, and severity level.

2. Syslog - This table contains security-related events and other system events that are generated by Linux and other Unix-based operating systems. The table includes information about the event, such as the facility and severity level.

Reference:

https://docs.microsoft.com/en-us/azure/azure-monitor/platform/data-sources-windows-events https://docs.microsoft.com/en-us/azure/azure-monitor/agents/data-sources-syslog

https://learn.microsoft.com/en-us/azure/azure-monitor/agents/data-sources-windows-events#log-queries-with-windows-events

11) CEF

When designing a large Azure environment with multiple subscriptions and planning to use Azure Policy as part of a governance solution, you can assign Azure Policy definitions at the following three scopes:

C. Subscriptions

Explanation: Azure Policy can be assigned at the subscription level, allowing you to enforce policies across the entire subscription.

E. Resource groups

Explanation: Azure Policy can be assigned at the resource group level, enabling you to enforce policies for specific sets of resources within a subscription.

F. Management groups

Explanation: Azure Policy can be assigned at the management group level, providing a way to enforce policies across multiple subscriptions that are organized under the same management group.

So, the correct answer is C, E, and F.

If you go into the portal and look at the scope section when assigning a policy it gives you the options of management group, subscription and resource group.

Reference:

https://docs.microsoft.com/en-us/azure/azure-resource-manager/management/overview#understand-scope

https://docs.microsoft.com/en-us/azure/governance/policy/overview

https://docs.microsoft.com/en-us/azure/governance/policy/concepts/scope

12)

1. Azure AD App Proxy

2. Azure AD enterprise app

3. Conditional Access policy

https://learn.microsoft.com/en-us/azure/active-directory/app-proxy/application-proxy-add-on-premises-application

https://learn.microsoft.com/en-us/azure/active-directory/app-proxy/application-proxy

Azure Active Directory's Application Proxy provides secure remote access to on-premises web applications. After a single sign-on to Azure AD, users can access both cloud and on-premises applications through an external URL or an internal application portal.

Azure AD Application Proxy is:

- Secure. On-premises applications can use Azure's authorization controls and security analytics. For example, on-premises applications can use Conditional Access and two-step verification. Application Proxy doesn't require you to open inbound connections through your firewall.

Step 1: Azure AD Application Proxy

Start by enabling communication to Azure data centers to prepare your environment for Azure AD Application Proxy.

Step 2: an Azure AD enterprise application

Add an on-premises app to Azure AD.

Now that you've prepared your environment and installed a connector, you're ready to add on-premises applications to Azure AD.

1. Sign in as an administrator in the Azure portal.

2. In the left navigation panel, select Azure Active Directory.

3. Select Enterprise applications, and then select new

application.

4. Etc.

Reference:

https://docs.microsoft.com/en-us/azure/active-directory/app-proxy/application-proxy-add-on-premises-application

13) A

A. Azure Activity Log

The Azure Activity Log provides insights into subscription-level events that have occurred in Azure. It can be used to monitor the operations performed on resources in the subscription, including when resources are created or modified. You can create a Log Analytics workspace and configure a log query to retrieve the details of new resource deployments for a given time range. This query can then be scheduled to run monthly and generate a report of new ARM resource deployments.

Activity logs are kept for 90 days. You can query for any range of dates, as long as the starting date isn't more than 90 days in the past.

Through activity logs, you can determine:

∽ what operations were taken on the resources in your subscription

∽ who started the operation

∽ when the operation occurred

∽ the status of the operation

∽ the values of other properties that might help you research the operation

Reference:

https://docs.microsoft.com/en-us/azure/azure-resource-manager/management/view-activity-logs

14) B

Answer: B. No

The described approach does not directly address the goal of identifying whether packets are being allowed or denied to the virtual machines. The Azure Monitoring agent and Dependency Agent primarily focus on monitoring and dependency tracking, which helps in understanding application performance and dependencies.

To specifically analyze network traffic, you might consider using Azure Network Watcher or tools like Network Performance Monitor (NPM). These tools are designed for network monitoring and troubleshooting, allowing you to capture and analyze network traffic, identify connectivity issues, and determine if packets are being allowed or denied.

In summary, while Azure Monitor and its agents are valuable for various aspects of monitoring, for in-depth network analysis, you would typically leverage dedicated network monitoring tools like Azure Network Watcher or Network Performance Monitor.

Use the Azure Monitor agent if you need to:

Collect guest logs and metrics from any machine in Azure, in other clouds, or on-premises.

Use the Dependency agent if you need to:

Use the Map feature VM insights or the Service Map solution.

Note: Instead use Azure Network Watcher IP Flow Verify allows you to detect traffic filtering issues at a VM level.

IP flow verify checks if a packet is allowed or denied to or from a virtual machine. The information consists of direction, protocol, local IP, remote IP, local port, and remote port. If the packet is denied by a security group, the name of the rule that denied the packet is returned. While any source or destination IP can be chosen,

IP flow verify helps administrators quickly diagnose connectivity issues from or to the internet and from or to the on-premises environment.

Azure Network Watcher IP Flow Verify, which allows you to detect traffic filtering issues at a VM level.

Reference:

https://docs.microsoft.com/en-us/azure/network-watcher/network-watcher-ip-flow-verify-overview

https://docs.microsoft.com/en-us/azure/network-watcher/network-watcher-ip-flow-verify-overview https://docs.microsoft.com/en-us/azure/azure-monitor/agents/agents-overview#dependency-agent

15)

1. Event Hub: You can export AD logs to an Azure Event Hub (even you can cherry picking which ones)

You can route Azure Active Directory (Azure AD) activity logs to several endpoints for long term retention and data insights.

The Event Hub is used for streaming.

2. Azure Function: You easily create a serverless function to read events from the Event Hub and store them in a CosmosDB.

Use an Azure Function along with a cosmos DB change feed, and store the data in Cosmos DB.

Reference:

https://docs.microsoft.com/en-us/azure/active-directory/reports-monitoring/concept-activity-logs-azure-monitor

https://docs.microsoft.com/en-us/azure/azure-functions/functions-event-hub-cosmos-db?tabs=bash

https://docs.microsoft.com/en-us/azure/active-directory/reports-monitoring/tutorial-azure-monitor-stream-logs-to-event-hub

16) D

Solution: Azure API Management

Azure API Management can be used to address the requirements:

Requests Rate Limiting: Azure API Management allows you to apply rate limiting policies to control the rate at which requests are sent to your logic apps. This can be configured to ensure that requests from Fabrikam developers are limited to lower rates compared to Contoso users.

Third-Party OAuth 2.0 Provider: Azure API Management supports OAuth 2.0 authentication, allowing Fabrikam developers to use their existing OAuth 2.0 provider for authentication.

No Changes to Logic Apps: The solution involving Azure API Management doesn't require changes to the logic apps. You can configure the API Management policies to control access and rate limiting without modifying the logic apps themselves.

No Azure AD Guest Accounts: Azure API Management does not require Azure AD guest accounts, providing a solution that aligns with the specified requirement.

Therefore, the recommended solution is D. Azure API Management.

Many APIs support OAuth 2.0 to secure the API and ensure that only valid users have access, and they can only access resources to which they're entitled. To use Azure API Management's interactive developer console with such APIs, the service allows you to configure your service instance to work with your OAuth 2.0 enabled API.

Incorrect:

Azure AD business-to-business (B2B) uses guest accounts.

Azure AD Application Proxy is for on-premises scenarios.

Reference:

API management can use Oauth2 for authorization:

https://docs.microsoft.com/en-us/azure/api-management/authorizations-overview

17)

1. Log Analytics workspace

Send resource logs to a Log Analytics workspace to enable the features of Azure Monitor Logs.

You must create a diagnostic setting for each Azure resource to send its resource logs to a Log Analytics workspace to use with Azure Monitor Logs.

2. Install Azure Monitor agent

Use the Azure Monitor agent if you need to:

Collect guest logs and metrics from any machine in Azure, in other clouds, or on-premises.

Manage data collection configuration centrally.

https://learn.microsoft.com/en-us/azure/azure-monitor/logs/log-analytics-workspace-overview

A Log Analytics workspace is a unique environment for log data from Azure Monitor and other Azure services, such as Microsoft Sentinel and Microsoft Defender for Cloud. Each workspace has its own data repository and configuration but might combine data from multiple services.

https://learn.microsoft.com/en-us/azure/azure-monitor/agents/agents-overview

Azure Monitor Agent (AMA) collects monitoring data from the guest operating system of Azure and hybrid virtual machines and delivers it to Azure Monitor for use by features, insights, and other services, such as Microsoft Sentinel and Microsoft Defender for Cloud. Azure Monitor Agent replaces all of Azure Monitor's legacy monitoring agents.

18)

Box 1: Azure AD Privileged Identity Management

Privileged Identity Management provides time-based and approval-based role activation to mitigate the risks of excessive, unnecessary, or misused access permissions on resources that you care about. Here are some of the key features of Privileged Identity Management:

Provide just-in-time privileged access to Azure AD and Azure resources

Assign time-bound access to resources using start and end dates

Require approval to activate privileged roles

Enforce multi-factor authentication to activate any role

Use justification to understand why users activate

Get notifications when privileged roles are activated

Conduct access reviews to ensure users still need roles

Download audit history for internal or external audit

Prevents removal of the last active Global Administrator role assignment

Box 2: Azure Managed Identity -

Managed identities provide an identity for applications to use when connecting to resources that support Azure Active Directory (Azure AD) authentication.

Applications may use the managed identity to obtain Azure AD tokens. With Azure Key Vault, developers can use managed identities to access resources. Key

Vault stores credentials in a secure manner and gives access to storage accounts.

Box 3: Azure AD Privileged Identity Management

Privileged Identity Management provides time-based and approval-based role activation to mitigate the risks of excessive, unnecessary, or misused access permissions on resources that you care about. Here are some of the key features of Privileged Identity Management:

Provide just-in-time privileged access to Azure AD and Azure resources

Assign time-bound access to resources using start and end dates

Privileged Identity Management provides time-based and approval-based role activation to mitigate the risks of excessive, unnecessary, or misused access permissions on resources that you care about. Here are some of the key features of Privileged Identity Management:

Provide just-in-time privileged access to Azure AD and Azure resources.

Assign time-bound access to resources using start and end dates.

Require approval to activate privileged roles.

Enforce multi-factor authentication to activate any role.

Use justification to understand why users activate.

Get notifications when privileged roles are activated.

Conduct access reviews to ensure users still need roles.

Download audit history for internal or external audit.

Prevents removal of the last active Global Administrator and Privileged Role Administrator role assignments.

Reference:

https://learn.microsoft.com/en-us/azure/active-directory/privileged-identity-management/pim-configure

https://docs.microsoft.com/en-us/azure/active-directory/managed-identities-azure-resources/overview

19)

The answer is 2-2-2

- 1 management group in each tenant: 2 in total.

- 1 definition in each tenant (you can't share the definition): 2 in total.

- you'll need to assign the definition in each tenant to the MG in the same tenant: 2 in total.

Blueprint can be assigned to MG level although the following statement from Azure docs is confusing:

"Assigning a blueprint definition to a management group means the assignment object exists at the management group. The deployment of artifacts still targets a subscription"

Reference:

https://docs.microsoft.com/en-us/azure/governance/blueprints/overview

20)

1. Modify

Modify is used to add, update, or remove properties or tags on a subscription or resource during creation or update. A common example is updating tags on resources such as costCenter. Existing non-compliant resources can be remediated with a remediation task. A single Modify rule can have any number of operations. Policy assignments with effect set as Modify require a managed identity to do remediation.

Incorrect:

* The following effects are deprecated: EnforceOPAConstraint EnforceRegoPolicy

* Append is used to add additional fields to the requested resource during creation or update. A common example is specifying allowed IPs for a storage resource.

Append is intended for use with non-tag properties. While Append can add tags to a resource during a create or update request, it's recommended to use the

Modify effect for tags instead.

2. Managed identity with Contributor role

The managed identity needs to be granted the appropriate roles required for remediating resources to grant the managed identity.

Contributor - Can create and manage all types of Azure resources but can't grant access to others.

Incorrect:

User Access Administrator: lets you manage user access to Azure resources.

Reference:

https://learn.microsoft.com/en-us/azure/governance/policy/concepts/effects#modify

21)

1: Yes -

A single diagnostic setting can define no more than one of each of the destinations. If you want to send data to more than one of a particular destination type (for example, two different Log Analytics workspaces), then create multiple settings.

Each resource can have up to 5 diagnostic settings.

Note: This diagnostic telemetry can be streamed to one of the following Azure resources for analysis.

* Log Analytics workspace

* Azure Event Hubs

* Azure Storage

2: Yes

3: Yes

Platform logs and metrics can be sent to the destinations listed in the following table.

- Log Analytics workspace

- Azure Storage account

- Azure Event Hubs

- Azure Monitor partner integrations

Reference:

https://docs.microsoft.com/en-us/azure/azure-monitor/essentials/diagnostic-settings

https://docs.microsoft.com/en-us/azure/azure-sql/database/metrics-diagnostic-telemetry-logging-streaming-export-configure?tabs=azure-portal

22) A

A. dynamic data masking

Dynamic Data Masking (DDM) is a feature in Azure SQL Database that helps you protect sensitive data by obfuscating it from non-privileged users. DDM allows you to define masking rules on specific columns, so that the data in those columns is automatically replaced with a masked value when queried by users without the appropriate permissions. This ensures that only privileged users can view the actual Personally Identifiable Information (PII), while other users will see the masked data.

Dynamic data masking limits sensitive data exposure by masking it to non-privileged users.

Dynamic data masking helps prevent unauthorized access to sensitive data by enabling customers to designate how much of the sensitive data to reveal with minimal impact on the application layer. It's a policy-based security feature that hides the sensitive data in the result set of a query over designated database fields, while the data in the database is not changed.

Reference:

https://docs.microsoft.com/en-us/azure/azure-sql/database/dynamic-data-masking-overview

https://docs.microsoft.com/en-us/sql/relational-databases/security/dynamic-data-masking?view=sql-server-ver16

23) B

B. blobs in a general purpose v2 storage account

A General Purpose v2 (GPv2) storage account can store blobs, files, queues, and tables, making it a versatile option for a wide range of applications. It supports customer-managed keys for encryption, allowing you to maintain control over the encryption keys.

To encrypt each user's data with a separate key, you can use Azure Blob Storage Service Encryption with customer-managed keys, storing each user's data in separate containers, and then configuring separate encryption keys for each container.

You can specify a customer-provided key on Blob storage operations. A client making a read or write request against Blob storage can include an encryption key on the request for granular control over how blob data is encrypted and decrypted.

Reference:

https://docs.microsoft.com/en-us/azure/storage/common/storage-service-encryption

https://learn.microsoft.com/en-us/azure/storage/common/storage-service-encryption#about-encryption-key-management

24)

1. Key Vault references in Application settings.

Source Application Settings from Key Vault.

Key Vault references can be used as values for Application Settings, allowing you to keep secrets in Key Vault instead of the site config. Application Settings are securely encrypted at rest, but if you need secret management capabilities, they should go into Key Vault.

To use a Key Vault reference for an app setting, set the reference as the value of the setting. Your app can reference the secret through its key as normal. No code changes are required.

2. Secrets: Get

In order to read secrets from Key Vault, you need to have a vault created and give your app permission to access it.

1. Create a key vault by following the Key Vault quickstart.

2. Create a managed identity for your application.

3. Key Vault references will use the app's system assigned identity by default, but you can specify a user-assigned identity.

4. Create an access policy in Key Vault for the application identity you created earlier. Enable the "Get" secret permission on this policy.

https://learn.microsoft.com/en-us/azure/app-service/app-service-key-vault-references?tabs=azure-cli#source-application-settings-from-key-vault

Key Vault references can be used as values for Application Settings, allowing you to keep secrets in Key Vault instead of the site config. Application Settings are securely encrypted at rest, but if you need secret management capabilities, they should go into Key Vault.

To use a Key Vault reference for an app setting, set the reference as the value of the setting. Your app can reference the secret through its key as normal. No code changes are required.

https://learn.microsoft.com/en-us/azure/app-service/app-service-key-vault-references?tabs=azure-cli#granting-your-app-access-to-key-vault

Create an access policy in Key Vault for the application identity you created earlier. Enable the "Get" secret permission on this policy. Do not configure the "authorized application" or applicationId settings, as this is not compatible with a managed identity.

25) D

D. a user-assigned managed identity

A user-assigned managed identity is the best choice for this scenario. User-assigned managed identities are standalone Azure Active Directory (Azure AD) identities that can be assigned to one or more Azure resources, such as virtual machines. They can be used to authenticate to other Azure services like Azure Key Vault, Azure Logic Apps instances, and Azure SQL Database without the need for storing secrets and certificates on the virtual machines.

By using a user-assigned managed identity, you can easily assign the same identity to multiple virtual machines, which avoids assigning new roles and permissions when you deploy additional VMs. This also minimizes administrative effort in managing identities, as the managed identity is automatically managed by Azure AD.

Managed identities provide an identity for applications to use when connecting to resources that support Azure Active Directory (Azure AD) authentication.

A user-assigned managed identity:

Can be shared.

The same user-assigned managed identity can be associated with more than one Azure resource.

Common usage:

Workloads that run on multiple resources and can share a single identity.

For example, a workload where multiple virtual machines need to access the same resource.

Incorrect:

Not A: A system-assigned managed identity can't be shared. It can only be associated with a single Azure resource.

Typical usage:

Workloads that are contained within a single Azure resource.

Workloads for which you need independent identities.

For example, an application that runs on a single virtual machine.

Reference:

https://docs.microsoft.com/en-us/azure/active-directory/managed-identities-azure-resources/overview

26) C

Azure Synapse Link for Azure Cosmos DB creates a tight integration between Azure Cosmos DB and Azure Synapse Analytics. It enables customers to run near real-time analytics over their operational data with full performance isolation from their transactional workloads and without an ETL pipeline.

Azure Synapse Link for Azure Cosmos DB is a cloud-native hybrid transactional and analytical processing (HTAP) capability that enables near real time analytics over operational data in Azure Cosmos DB. Azure Synapse Link creates a tight seamless integration between Azure Cosmos DB and Azure Synapse Analytics.

Reference:

https://learn.microsoft.com/en-us/azure/cosmos-db/synapse-link

27) Correct answer is 90 and 730.

To those who say infinite: You may be thinking that the 90 days is how long it's storing the data "somewhere" before archiving to the storage account. This is not correct. The retention time boxes only appear after you select the "archive to storage account" checkbox. This retention period is applying specifically to the data in the storage account.

1. The amount of time that SQLInsights data will be stored in blob storage - yes, the 'maximum' is infinite, but 90 days has been selected in the diagram.

2. Second question is asking the 'maximum', so that answer is 730.

Reference:

https://docs.microsoft.com/en-us/azure/azure-monitor/app/data-retention-privacy

28) C

Password-based - Choose password-based when the application has an HTML sign-in page. Password-based SSO is also known as password vaulting. Password-based SSO enables you to manage user access and passwords to web applications that don't support identity federation. It's also useful where several users need to share a single account, such as to your organization's social media app accounts.

Password-based SSO supports applications that require multiple sign-in fields for applications that require more than just username and password fields to sign in. You can customize the labels of the username and password fields your users see on My Apps when they enter their credentials.

Reference:

https://learn.microsoft.com/en-us/azure/active-directory/manage-apps/plan-sso-deployment#single-sign-on-options

https://learn.microsoft.com/en-us/azure/active-directory/manage-apps/plan-sso-deployment#single-sign-on-options

29)

1. Azure Bastion.

It provides secure and seamless RDP/SSH connectivity to your virtual machines directly from the Azure portal over TLS.

While JIT access allows access via RDP or SSH, incoming connections is not TLS tcp 443 (but RDP or SSH when the inbound port is temporarily authorized)

https://docs.microsoft.com/en-us/azure/defender-for-cloud/just-in-time-access-usage?tabs=jit-config-avm%2Cjit-request-asc

https://docs.microsoft.com/en-us/azure/bastion/bastion-overview

2. A conditional Access policy that has Cloud Apps assignment set to Azure Windows VM Sign-In

Enforce Conditional Access policies

You can enforce Conditional Access policies, such as multifactor authentication or user sign-in risk check, before you authorize access to Windows VMs in Azure that are enabled with Azure AD login. To apply a Conditional Access policy, you must select the

Azure Windows VM Sign-In app from the cloud apps or actions assignment option. Then use sign-in risk as a condition and/or require MFA as a control for granting access.

https://docs.microsoft.com/en-us/azure/active-directory/devices/howto-vm-sign-in-azure-ad-windows

30) C

To ensure that you can easily identify Azure resources based on operational information and use this information when generating reports, you should include the following in the solution:

C. Enforce tagging rules using an Azure policy.

By enforcing tagging rules, you can consistently apply metadata (such as environment, owner, department, and cost center) to Azure resources, making it easier to categorize and report on them.

You apply tags to your Azure resources, resource groups, and subscriptions to logically organize them into a taxonomy. Each tag consists of a name and a value pair.

You use Azure Policy to enforce tagging rules and conventions. By creating a policy, you avoid the scenario of resources being deployed to your subscription that don't have the expected tags for your organization. Instead of manually applying tags or searching for resources that aren't compliant, you create a policy that automatically applies the needed tags during deployment.

Reference:

https://docs.microsoft.com/en-us/azure/azure-resource-manager/management/tag-policies

31) D

Collaborate with any partner using their identities

With Azure AD B2B, the partner uses their own identity management solution, so there is no external administrative overhead for your organization. Guest users sign in to your apps and services with their own work, school, or social identities.

The partner uses their own identities and credentials, whether or not they have an Azure AD account.

You don't need to manage external accounts or passwords.

You don't need to sync accounts or manage account lifecycles.

You can use the capabilities in Azure Active Directory B2B to collaborate with external guest users and you can use Azure RBAC to grant just the permissions that guest users need in your environment.

Incorrect:

Not B: Forest trust is used for internal security, not external access.

Reference:

https://docs.microsoft.com/en-us/azure/role-based-access-control/role-assignments-external-users

https://docs.microsoft.com/en-us/azure/active-directory/external-identities/what-is-b2b

32) C

The app is single tenant authentication so users must be present in contoso directory.

https://docs.microsoft.com/en-us/azure/active-directory/develop/single-and-multi-tenant-apps

With Azure AD B2B, external users authenticate to their home directory, but have a representation in your directory.

https://docs.microsoft.com/en-us/azure/active-directory/governance/entitlement-management-external-users

A is wrong because it's to automate provisioning to third party SaaS app.

https://docs.microsoft.com/en-us/azure/active-directory/app-provisioning/how-provisioning-works?source=recommendations

B. is wrong because the application would need to switch to multi-tenant.

https://docs.microsoft.com/en-us/azure/active-directory/develop/howto-convert-app-to-be-multi-tenant

IF App1 is multi-tenant application, A might be correct since you can provision users from other tenant to App1 and configure App1 to SSO with other tenants.

33)

1: Azure AD -

Grant permissions in Azure AD.

2: Azure API Management -

Configure a JWT validation policy to pre-authorize requests.

Pre-authorize requests in API Management with the Validate JWT policy, by validating the access tokens of each incoming request. If a request does not have a valid token, API Management blocks it.

Authorization workflow

A user or application acquires a token from Azure AD with permissions that grant access to the backend-app.

The token is added in the Authorization header of API requests to API Management.

API Management validates the token by using the validate-jwt policy.

If a request doesn't have a valid token, API Management blocks it.

If a request is accompanied by a valid token, the gateway can forward the request to the API.

Reference:

https://docs.microsoft.com/en-us/azure/api-management/api-management-access-restriction-policies#ValidateJWT

https://docs.microsoft.com/en-us/azure/api-management/api-management-howto-protect-backend-with-aad

34) A

To generate a monthly report of all new Azure Resource Manager (ARM) resource deployments in your Azure subscription, the recommended solution is:

A. Implement Azure Log Analytics.

Azure Log Analytics is a powerful tool for collecting, analyzing, and querying log data from various Azure resources, including Azure Resource Manager (ARM) deployments. By creating a custom query in Azure Log Analytics, you can generate a monthly report of all the new ARM resource deployments in your Azure subscription. This will allow you to monitor and analyze resource deployment activities and trends over time.

The Activity log is a platform log in Azure that provides insight into subscription-level events. Activity log includes such information as when a resource is modified or when a virtual machine is started.

Activity log events are retained in Azure for 90 days and then deleted.

For more functionality, you should create a diagnostic setting to send the Activity log to one or more of these locations for the following reasons: to Azure Monitor Logs for more complex querying and alerting, and longer retention (up to two years) to Azure Event Hubs to forward outside of Azure-to-Azure Storage for cheaper, long-term archiving

Note: Azure Monitor builds on top of Log Analytics, the platform service that gathers log and metrics data from all your resources. The easiest way to think about it is that Azure Monitor is the marketing name, whereas Log Analytics is the technology that powers it.

Reference:

https://docs.microsoft.com/en-us/azure/azure-monitor/essentials/activity-log

35) B

To generate compliance reports for an Azure subscription containing 1,000 resources, with the requirement to organize resources by department, what should you use?

B. Leverage Azure Policy and tags.

Using Azure Policy along with tags allows you to categorize and organize resources, making it easier to generate compliance reports based on your specific criteria.

"To organize the resources in your Azure subscription and generate compliance reports, you should use Azure Policy and tags.

Azure Policy allows you to define and enforce rules and regulations for your resources, ensuring compliance with organizational standards and industry regulations. You can create policies that specify the required tags for resources, such as department, and enforce their usage across the subscription. This will help you categorize and group resources based on departments.

Tags, on the other hand, are key-value pairs that you can assign to resources. By assigning tags to resources with the department information, you can easily filter and group resources based on departments when generating compliance reports.

Therefore, the correct answer is B. Azure Policy and tags."

36) B

To minimize administrative effort for authentication while developing an app that reads activity logs for an Azure subscription using Azure Functions, the recommended solution is:

B. Set up a system-assigned managed identity for Azure Functions.

System-assigned managed identities provide a way for Azure Functions to authenticate to other Azure services, such as Activity Logs, without the need for storing or managing secrets. This approach minimizes administrative effort because the identity is tied directly to the Azure Functions service and is automatically managed by Azure. When the Azure Functions instance is deleted, the associated managed identity will also be removed. This simplifies the authentication process and helps improve the security posture of your app.

Reference:

https://learn.microsoft.com/en-us/azure/active-directory/managed-identities-azure-resources/overview

37) C

Based on the requirements below:

The evaluation must be repeated automatically every three months.

• Every member must be able to report whether they need to be in Group1.

• Users who report that they do not need to be in Group1 must be removed from Group1 automatically.

• Users who do not report whether they need to be in Group1 must be removed from Group1 automatically.

Reference:

https://learn.microsoft.com/en-us/azure/active-directory/governance/access-reviews-overview

38) Important point here is that both apps are deployed to the same machines. So managed identity will violate the principle of least privilege. As a user/system managed identity will have to be assigned both read and write permission to user's calendar.

App registration will provide ability to use the service principal per app to set the correct permission required for the app.

Use delegated permissions to access user's data as admin allowed/forces users to delegate the permission to the app.

answer:

1. App registration

2. Delegated permissions

39) Yes, No, Yes

Since Group 1 is assigned VM contributor to MG1, it will be able to create a new VM in RG1.

User 2 is not able to grant permission to Group 2 because it is just a member with contributor role.

Since Group 3 has Contributor role for the Tenant Root Group, User3 can create storage account in RG2

user1 can create a new virtual machine in rg1 because they are a member of Group1, which has the Virtual Machine Contributor role for MG1, and rg1 is under sub1.

user2 cannot grant permissions to group2 because they only have the Contributor role and not the necessary administrative role for group2.

user3 cannot create a storage account in rg2 because although Group3 has the Contributor role for the Tenant Root Group, user3 needs to be assigned a specific role that allows them to create storage accounts. Being a member of Group1 and Group2 does not provide the authority to create a storage account in rg2.

40)

1. Client credentials grant flows

2. Azure Instance Metadata (IMDS) endpoint

The key difference in this scenario is that we are using a Managed Identity, which is a feature of Azure AD, and in that case, access tokens are obtained through the Azure Instance Metadata Service (IMDS) API. The managed identity is responsible for managing the lifecycle of these credentials.

Therefore, for the case of an application in an Azure VM that uses a managed identity to authenticate with Key Vault, the IMDS would be used, not an OAuth 2.0 endpoint directly.

Reference:

https://docs.microsoft.com/en-us/azure/active-directory/managed-identities-azure-resources/how-to-use-vm-token#get-a-token-using-http

41) D

To generate a monthly report of all new Azure Resource Manager (ARM) resource deployments in your Azure subscription, you should include the following recommendation:

D. Azure Log Analytics

Explanation:

Azure Log Analytics provides a centralized and flexible platform for collecting and analyzing telemetry data from Azure resources. By using Azure Resource Manager (ARM) logs, you can track resource deployments, modifications, and deletions. Azure Log Analytics allows you to query and analyze this data, making it suitable for generating reports on resource deployment activities.

Options B (Azure Monitor metrics) and C (Azure Advisor) are not specifically designed for tracking resource deployments. Azure Monitor metrics focus on performance and health data, while Azure Advisor provides best practices and recommendations for improving resources but does not directly address deployment reporting.

Option A (Azure Arc) is not directly related to generating reports on resource deployments within an Azure subscription. Azure Arc is a service that extends Azure management capabilities to on-premises, multi-cloud environments, and edge devices.

42) 1) c, 2) a

The roles that you need to assign are:

User1: User Administrator for the MarketingAU administrative unit.

User2: Password Administrator or Helpdesk Administrator for the MarketingAU administrative unit.

The User Administrator role provides permissions to manage user accounts, including creating new users. The Password Administrator and Helpdesk Administrator roles provide permissions to reset user passwords.

Therefore, User1 needs the User Administrator role for the

MarketingAU administrative unit to be able to create new user accounts. User2 needs either the Password Administrator or Helpdesk Administrator role for the MarketingAU administrative unit to be able to reset user passwords.

Note that assigning Helpdesk Administrator for the tenant role to User2 would provide permissions to reset passwords for all users in the Azure AD tenant, not just in the MarketingAU administrative unit.

Reference:

https://learn.microsoft.com/en-us/azure/active-directory/roles/admin-units-assign-roles

43)

1. Storage: c. Secret.

API keys are typically stored as secrets in Azure Key Vault. The key vault can store and manage secrets like API keys, passwords, or database connection strings.

2. Access: b. A managed service identity (MSI).

A managed service identity (MSI) is used to give your VM access to the key vault. The advantage of using MSI is that you do not have to manage credentials yourself. Azure takes care of rolling the credentials and ensuring their lifecycle. The application running on your VM can use its managed service identity to get a token to Azure AD, and then use that token to authenticate to Azure Key Vault.

44)

1. App1: b. App roles

2. App2: c. Token configuration

This is assuming that the exam expects you to know that an application requesting a token (App2) would need to have the roles claim added via Token Configuration. While in practice, this is not the exact place to assign a role to an application, but given the choices provided, this would be the most appropriate.

This is because token configuration does indeed impact the claims present in a token, and since no other suitable choice is available (API Permissions would not be used to assign a role to the application), it seems this would be the expected answer.

However, please note this is not entirely accurate based on the full capabilities of Azure AD, but it's the best choice given the options. Normally, you would assign the app role to the service principal of App2 in the context of Enterprise Applications, which is not an option here.

To ensure that when App2 authenticates to access App1, the tokens issued by Azure AD include the Writer role claim:

1. In the Azure portal, navigate to Azure Active Directory > App registrations.

2. Select App1.

3. Under Manage, select App roles.

4. Select New app role.

5. In the Name field, enter Writer.

6. In the Description field, enter a description of the Writer role.

7. Select Create.

8. Select App2.

9. Under Manage, select Token configuration.

10. In the Issued token claims section, select Add claim.

11. In the Name field, enter roles.

12. In the Source field, select Application.

13. In the Value field, enter Writer.

14. Select Add.

15. Select Save.

Once you have completed these steps, when App2 authenticates to access App1, the tokens issued by Azure AD will include the Writer role claim.

Note: For native applications, such as App2, you cannot use the Manifest blade to add the Writer role claim. Instead, you must use the Token configuration blade.

45) A

Based on the information provided, the minimum number of Azure Monitor workspaces required is 1.

The key points:

Azure Monitor Network Insights, Application Insights, Microsoft Sentinel, and VM insights can all be enabled within a single Azure Monitor workspace.

Azure Monitor workspaces allow you to organize and manage monitoring data, configurations, and analytics.

Since a single team will be managing the monitoring solution, a single workspace is sufficient. Multiple workspaces are only needed if you want to divide management responsibilities.

All the mentioned monitoring services can be integrated into the same workspace. For example, you can ingest network and application logs into Microsoft Sentinel enabled in that workspace.

VM insights can also be configured for the VMs to send data to the same workspace.

Application Insights and Network Insights are natively integrated into the workspace.

Minimum: 1

Ideal: 2

1 workspace for Azure Monitor Network Insights. This workspace will collect and store network telemetry data from your Azure resources.

1 workspace for Application Insights, Microsoft Sentinel, and VM insights. This workspace will collect and store application, security, and virtual machine telemetry data from your Azure resources.

By doing this, you can:

Improve performance. By separating the different types of telemetry data, you can optimize the performance of your queries.

Improve security. By separating the different types of telemetry data, you can reduce the risk of unauthorized access.

Improve compliance. By separating the different types of telemetry data, you can make it easier to comply with regulatory requirements.

Reference:

https://learn.microsoft.com/en-us/azure/azure-monitor/logs/workspace-design

46)

1. 1 AAD now Microsoft Entra ID

2. 2 Conditional access policies:

- Conditional Access Policy for Admin Access to the Azure Portal

- Conditional Access Policy for Testing WebApp1 Updates

• All administrative access to the Azure portal must be secured by using multi-factor authentication (MFA).

• The testing of WebApp1 updates must not be visible to anyone outside the company.

47) D

D. Microsoft Entra ID Governance

Explanation: Leveraging Microsoft Entra ID Governance provides the capability to implement access management policies and lifecycle management for users. This solution aligns with the requirement of restricting users to access only the app associated with their current project. Additionally, it enables project managers to verify and manage user access, meeting the criteria of project managers being able to review and remove users not assigned to their projects. Microsoft Entra ID Governance can also automate access reviews, addressing the need for project managers to be prompted every 30 days to verify user assignments.

48)

1: DeployIfNotExists

DeployIfNotExists policy definition executes a template deployment when the condition is met. Policy assignments with effect set as DeployIfNotExists require a managed identity to do remediation.

2: The role-based access control (RABC) roles required to

perform the remediation task

The question is what you have to "Include in the definition:" of the policy.

Refer to list of DeployIfNotExists properties, among them is roleDefinitionIds (required) - This property must include an array of strings that match role-based access control role ID accessible by the subscription.

Reference:

https://learn.microsoft.com/en-us/azure/governance/policy/concepts/effects#deployifnotexists

49) B

You should include the following in the solution:

B. Application Insights

Explanation:

Application Insights is the Azure service designed for monitoring and gaining insights into the performance and usage of your applications. It can be particularly effective for tracking the behavior and performance of distributed applications, such as those using containers.

Application Insights includes features for synthetic transaction monitoring, allowing you to create and run tests that mimic user interactions with your application. This aligns with the requirement to monitor traffic between App1 components using synthetic transactions.

Application Insights provides detailed telemetry data, including traces, exceptions, and performance metrics, minimizing development effort by offering a comprehensive monitoring solution out of the box.

Therefore, Application Insights is the suitable Azure Monitor component to meet the specified requirements for monitoring App1.

Reference:

https://azure.microsoft.com/en-us/updates/generally-available-application-insights-synthetic-monitoring-sla-report-template/

50) 1) c, 2) a

Since you have an average of 120GB of log data per day,

to minimize costs and impact you should to change the "Workspace1" plan from "pay-as-you-go" to "commitment pricing tier";

the "commitment pricing tier" is good starting at 100GB per day of logs.

"In addition to the pay-as-you-go model, Log Analytics has commitment tiers, which can save you as much as 30 percent compared to the pay-as-you-go price. With commitment tier pricing, you can commit to buy data ingestion for a workspace, starting at 100 GB per day, at a lower price than pay-as-you-go pricing."

Reference:

https://learn.microsoft.com/en-us/azure/azure-monitor/logs/cost-logs#commitment-tiers

PRACTICE TEST II

1) You have 12 Azure subscriptions and three projects.

Each project uses resources across multiple subscriptions.

You need to use Microsoft Cost Management to monitor costs on a per project basis. The solution must minimize administrative effort.

Which two components should you include in the solution?

A. budgets

B. resource tags

C. custom role-based access control (RBAC) roles

D. management groups

E. Azure boards

2) You have an Azure subscription with several storage accounts, and Azure Policy definitions are assigned to these accounts. Your task is to provide recommendations to meet the following criteria:

Initiate Azure Policy compliance scans on-demand.

Generate Azure Monitor alerts for non-compliance by querying logs collected through Log Analytics.

What solutions would you suggest for each requirement?

Please choose the suitable options in the answer area.

Answer area:

1) To trigger the compliance scans, use:

a. An Azure template

b. The Azure Command-Line Interface (CLI)

c. The Azure portal

2) To generate the non-compliance alerts, configure diagnostic settings for the:

a. Azure activity logs

b. Log Analytics workspace

c. Storage accounts

3) HOTSPOT:

In your Azure subscription, you intend to deploy five storage accounts for block blobs and five storage accounts for hosting file shares accessed via the SMB protocol. Your goal is to recommend an access authorization solution that adheres to the following requirements:

> • **Maximize security.**
> • **Avoid the use of shared keys.**
> • **Whenever feasible, support time-limited access.**

Provide your suggestions for the solution by selecting the appropriate options in the answer area.

Answer area:

1) For the blobs:

a. A user delegation shared access signature (SAS) only

b. A shared access signature (SAS) and a stored access policy

c. A user delegation shared access signature (SAS) and a stored access policy

2) For the file shares:

a. Azure AD credentials

b. A user delegation shared access signature (SAS) only

c. A user delegation shared access signature (SAS) and a stored access policy

4) HOTSPOT:

In your Azure subscription, there are 100 virtual machines running Windows Server 2022 with the Azure Monitor Agent installed. Your task is to provide a recommendation that fulfills the following criteria:

- Forward JSON-formatted logs from the virtual machines to a Log Analytics workspace.
- Transform the logs and store the data in a table within the Log Analytics workspace.

Offer your suggestions for the solution by selecting the appropriate options in the answer area.

Answer area:

1) To forward the logs:

a. A linked storage account for the Log Analytics workspace

b. An Azure Monitor data collection endpoint

c. A service endpoint

2) To transform the logs and store the data:

a. A KQL query

b. A WQL query

c. A XPAth query

5) HOTSPOT:

You have five Azure subscriptions, each associated with a distinct Azure AD tenant, and hosting virtual machines running Windows Server 2022.

You plan to collect Windows security events from the virtual machines and send them to a single Log Analytics workspace.

Your objective is to propose a solution that aligns with the following requirements:

· Collects event logs from multiple subscriptions

· Supports the use of data collection rules (DCRs) to define which events to collect

Provide your recommendations for each requirement by selecting the appropriate options in the answer area.

Answer area:

1) To collect the event logs:

a. Azure Event Grid

b. Azure Lighthouse

c. Azure Purview

2) To support the DCRs:

a. The Log Analytics agent

b. The Azure Monitor agent

c. the Azure Connected machine agent

6) You have 100 servers running Windows Server 2012 R2, each hosting Microsoft SQL Server 2014 instances with databases characterized by CLR-based stored procedures. The largest database is currently 3 TB, and it is ensured that no database will exceed 4 TB. Your objective is to propose a service for hosting these databases in Azure with the following requirements:

- **Minimize management overhead for the migrated databases whenever possible.**
- **Enable user authentication using Azure Active Directory (Azure AD) credentials.**
- **Minimize the required database changes for a smooth migration.**

What service should you recommend?

A. Azure SQL Database elastic pools

B. Azure SQL Managed Instance

C. Azure SQL Database single databases

D. SQL Server 2016 on Azure virtual machines

7) In your Azure subscription, there is an Azure Blob Storage account named store1. Concurrently, you have an on-premises file server, Server1, running Windows Server 2016 and housing 500 GB of company files.

Your objective is to create a duplicate of the company files from Server1 within store1. What are two potential Azure services that can accomplish this task?

A. an Azure Logic Apps integration account

B. an Azure Import/Export job

C. Azure Data Factory

D. an Azure Analysis services On-premises data gateway

E. an Azure Batch account

8) You have an Azure subscription with two applications, App1 and App2. App1 is a sales processing application that adds messages to an Azure Storage account queue when shipping is required. App2 listens to this queue for relevant transactions. You anticipate adding more applications in the future to process specific shipping requests.

You need to suggest an alternative to the storage account queue to ensure that each new application can read pertinent transactions.

What recommendation should you provide?

A. one Azure Data Factory pipeline

B. multiple storage account queues

C. one Azure Service Bus queue

D. one Azure Service Bus topic

9) HOTSPOT:

You need to design a storage solution for an app that will store large amounts of frequently used data. The solution must meet the following requirements:

∞ **Maximize data throughput.**

∞ **Prevent the modification of data for one year.**

∞ **Minimize latency for read and write operations.**

Which Azure Storage account type and storage service should you recommend?

To answer, choose the appropriate options in the answer area.

Hot Area:

Answer area:

1) Storage account type:

a. BlobStorage

b. BlockBlobStorage

c. FileStorage

d. StorageV2 with Premium performance

e. StorageV2 with Standard performance

2) Storage service:

a. Blob

b. File

c. Table

10) HOTSPOT:

You have an Azure subscription that contains the storage accounts shown in the following table.

Name	Type	Performance
storage1	StorageV2	Standard
storage2	StorageV2	Premium
storage3	BlobStorage	Standard
storage4	FileStorage	Premium

You plan to implement two new apps that have the requirements shown in the following table.

Name	Requirement
App1	Use lifecycle management to migrate app data between storage tiers
App2	Store app data in an Azure file share

Which storage accounts should you recommend using for each app?

To answer, choose the appropriate options in the answer area.

Hot Area:

Answer area:

1) App1:

a. Storage1 and Storage2 only

b. Storage1 and Storage3 only

c. Storage1, Storage2 and Storage3 only

d. Storage1, Storage2, Storage3 and Storage4

2) App2:

a. Storage4 only

b. Storage1 and Storage4 only

c. Storage1, Storage2 and Storage4 only

d. Storage1, Storage2, Storage3 and Storage4

11) You are developing an application to be hosted in Azure that will store video files ranging from 50 MB to 12 GB. The application will utilize certificate-based authentication and be accessible to internet users.

You need to suggest a storage option for the video files that offers optimal read performance and minimizes storage costs.

What is your recommendation?

A. Azure Files

B. Azure Data Lake Storage Gen2

C. Azure Blob Storage

D. Azure SQL Database

12) You are planning a SQL database solution that encompasses 20 databases, each with a size of 20 GB and exhibiting diverse usage patterns. Your goal is to suggest a database platform that aligns with the following requirements:

- **Achieve a Service Level Agreement (SLA) of 99.99% uptime.**
- **Dynamically scale compute resources allocated to the databases.**
- **Incorporate reserved capacity for the solution.**
- **Minimize compute charges.**

What would be your recommendation?

A. an elastic pool that contains 20 Azure SQL databases

B. 20 databases on a Microsoft SQL server that runs on an Azure virtual machine in an availability set

C. 20 databases on a Microsoft SQL server that runs on an Azure virtual machine

D. 20 instances of Azure SQL Database serverless

13) HOTSPOT:

You are tasked with designing the database architecture for migrating an on-premises database to Azure.

The design must adhere to specific requirements, including the ability to scale up and down, facilitate geo-redundant backups, handle a database size of up to 75 TB, and be optimized for online transaction processing (OLTP).

Choose the appropriate options from the answer area to fulfill these criteria.

Hot area:

Answer area:

1) Service:

a. Azure SQL Database

b. Azure SQL Managed Instance

c. Azure Synapse Analytics

d. SQL Server on Azure Virtual Machines

2) Service tier:

a. Basic

b. Business Critical

c. General Purpose

d. Hyperscale

e. Premium

f. Standard

14) You are devising an Azure IoT Hub solution with 50,000 IoT devices, each streaming data containing temperature, device ID, and time information.

Approximately 50,000 records will be generated every second, and the data needs to be visualized in near real time.

To store and query this data, you need to suggest two services.

Identify the suitable options from the following:

A. Azure Table Storage

B. Azure Event Grid

C. Azure Cosmos DB SQL API

D. Azure Time Series Insights

15) You're tasked with suggesting a database solution for an application that aggregates content for users. The chosen solution should adhere to the following criteria:

- **Support SQL commands.**
- **Support multi-master writes.**
- **Guarantee low latency for read operations.**

What recommendation do you propose?

A. Azure Cosmos DB SQL API

B. Azure SQL Database that uses active geo-replication

C. Azure SQL Database Hyperscale

D. Azure Database for PostgreSQL

16) HOTSPOT –

You have an Azure subscription that contains the SQL servers on Azure shown in the following table.

Name	Resource group	Location
SQLsvr1	RG1	East US
SQLsvr2	RG2	West US

The subscription contains the storage accounts shown in the following table.

Name	Resource group	Location	Account kind
storage1	RG1	East US	StorageV2 (general purposev2)
storage2	RG2	Central US	BlobStorage

You create the Azure SQL databases shown in the following table.

Name	Resource group	Server	Pricing tier
SQLdb1	RG1	SQLsvr1	Standard
SQLdb2	RG1	SQLsvr1	Standard
SQLdb3	RG2	SQLsvr2	Premium

For each of the following statements, select Yes if the statement is true. Otherwise, select No.

Hot Area:

Answer area:

Statements:

1) When you enable auditing for SQLdb1, you can store the audit information to storage1.

2) When you enable auditing for SQLdb2, you can store the audit information to storage2.

3) When you enable auditing for SQLdb3, you can store the audit information to storage3.

17) DRAG DROP:

You plan to import data from your on-premises environment to Azure. The data is shown in the following table.

On-premises source	Azure target
A Microsoft SQL Server 2012 database	An Azure SQL database
A table in a Microsoft SQL Server 2014 database	An Azure Cosmos DB account that uses the SQL API

What should you recommend using to migrate the data? To answer, drag the appropriate tools to the correct data sources.

Each tool may be used once, more than once, or not at all.

Select and Place:

Tools:

a. AzCopy

b. Azure Cosmos DB Data Migration Tool

c. Data Management Gateway

d. Data Migration Assistant

Answer area:

1) From the SQL Server 2012 database: ....

2) From the table in the SQL Server 2014 database: ....

18) You have web access logs stored in Azure Blob Storage and intend to create monthly reports from this data.

Your goal is to suggest an automated procedure for transferring the information to Azure SQL Database on a monthly basis.

What recommendation would you provide?

A. Microsoft SQL Server Migration Assistant (SSMA)

B. Data Migration Assistant (DMA)

C. AzCopy

D. Azure Data Factory

19) You possess an Azure subscription, and your on-premises network holds a file server named Server1 containing 5 terabytes of company files seldom accessed.

Your intention is to transfer these files to Azure Storage. To fulfill the requirements of having the files available within 24 hours of request and minimizing storage costs, identify two viable storage solutions.

Each correct response provides a comprehensive solution.

A. Create an Azure Blob Storage account that is configured for the Cool default access tier. Create a blob container, copy the files to the blob container, and set each file to the Archive access tier.

B. Create a general-purpose v1 storage account. Create a blob container and copy the files to the blob container.

C. Create a general-purpose v2 storage account that is configured for the Cool default access tier. Create a file share in the storage account and copy the files to the file share.

D. Create a general-purpose v2 storage account that is configured for the Hot default access tier. Create a blob container, copy the files to the blob container, and set each file to the Archive access tier.

E. Create a general-purpose v1 storage account. Create a fie share in the storage account and copy the files to the file share.

20) You have an application named App1 that utilizes two on-premises Microsoft SQL Server databases named DB1 and DB2. The plan is to migrate DB1 and DB2 to Azure.

Your task is to suggest an Azure solution to host DB1 and DB2 while meeting the following criteria:

- **Support server-side transactions across DB1 and DB2.**
- **Minimize administrative effort for updating the solution.**

What recommendation do you propose?

A. two Azure SQL databases in an elastic pool

B. two databases on the same Azure SQL managed instance

C. two databases on the same SQL Server instance on an Azure virtual machine

D. two Azure SQL databases on different Azure SQL Database servers

21) You are tasked with designing a highly available Azure SQL database with the following requirements:

- **Failover between replicas of the database must occur without any data loss.**
- **The database must remain available in the event of a zone outage.**
- **Costs must be minimized.**

Which deployment option would you recommend?

A. Azure SQL Database Hyperscale.

B. Azure SQL Database Premium.

C. Azure SQL Database Basic.

D. Azure SQL Managed Instance General Purpose.

22) HOTSPOT:

You are in the process of planning an Azure Storage solution for handling sensitive data that will be accessed daily. The dataset is less than 10 GB, and specific requirements need to be met:

- **All data written to storage must be retained for five years.**
- **Once the data is written, it can only be read, with modifications and deletions prohibited.**
- **After five years, the data can be deleted but not modified.**
- **Minimization of data access charges is essential.**

What recommendations should you propose?

Indicate the appropriate options in the answer area.

Hot area:

Answer area:

1) Storage account type:

a. General purpose v2 with archive access tier for blobs.

 b. General purpose v2 with Cool access tier for blobs.

 c. General purpose v2 with Hot access tier for blobs.

2) Configuration to prevent modifications and deletions:

a. Container access level

b. Container access policy

c. Storage account resource lock

23) HOTSPOT:

You are in the process of designing a data storage solution to facilitate reporting. The solution involves ingesting high volumes of data in JSON format through Azure Event Hubs, which then writes the data to storage. The solution must adhere to the following requirements:

- **Organize data in directories by date and time.**
- **Enable querying of stored data directly, transformation into summarized tables, and subsequent storage in a data warehouse.**
- **Ensure that the data warehouse can store 50 TB of relational data and support between 200 and 300 concurrent read operations.**

What services should be recommended for each type of data store?

Choose the appropriate options in the answer area.

Hot area:

Answer area:

1) Data store for the ingested data:

a. Azure Blob Storage

 b. Azure Data Lake Storage Gen2

c. Azure Files

d. Azure NetApp Files

2) Data store for the data warehouse:

 a. Azure Cosmos DB Cassandra API

b. Azure Cosmos DB SQL API

 c. Azure SQL Database Hyperscale

d. Azure Synapse Analytics dedicated SQL pools

24) You have an application called App1 that currently utilizes an on-premises Microsoft SQL Server database named DB1. The plan is to migrate DB1 to an Azure SQL managed instance.

Your goal is to enable customer-managed Transparent Data Encryption (TDE) for the instance while maximizing encryption strength.

What type of encryption algorithm and key length should you use for the TDE protector?

A. RSA 3072

B. AES 256

C. RSA 4096

D. RSA 2048

25) You are tasked with designing an Azure IoT Hub solution involving 50,000 IoT devices, each streaming data (temperature, device ID, and time) at a rate of approximately 50,000 records per second.

The data needs to be visualized in near real time. To store and query this data, you need to suggest two services.

Identify the suitable options, keeping in mind that each correct response provides a comprehensive solution.

A. Azure Table Storage

B. Azure Event Grid

C. Azure Cosmos DB for NoSQL

D. Azure Time Series Insights

26) You are devising an Azure Storage solution for handling sensitive data with daily access and a dataset size of less than 10 GB. The recommended storage solution should align with the following requirements:

- **Preserve all written data in storage for five years.**
- **Restrict the data to read-only access after being written, preventing modifications and deletions.**
- **Allow data deletion after five years without permitting modifications.**
- **Minimize data access charges.**

Choose the suitable options in the provided answer area.

Hot area:

Answer area:

1) Storage account type:

a. Premium block blobs

b. General purpose v2 with Cool access tier for blobs

c. General purpose v2 with Hot access tier for blobs

2) Configuration to prevent modifications and deletions:

a. Container access level

b. Container access policy

c. Storage account resource lock

27) You are devising an Azure Storage solution for handling sensitive data with daily access and a dataset size of less than 10 GB. The recommended storage solution should align with the following requirements:

- **Preserve all written data in storage for five years.**
- **Restrict the data to read-only access after being written, preventing modifications and deletions.**
- **Allow data deletion after five years without permitting modifications.**
- **Minimize data access charges.**

Choose the suitable options in the provided answer area.

Hot area:

Answer area:

1) Ingest data from Data Lake Storage into hash-distributed tables:

a. A dedicated SQL pool

b. A serverless Apache Spark pool

c. A serverless SQL pool

2) Implement, query, and update data in Delta Lake:

a. A dedicated SQL pool

b. A serverless Apache Spark pool

c. A serverless SQL pool

28) You possess an on-premises storage solution that needs migration to Azure. The migration must support the Hadoop Distributed File System (HDFS).

What Azure service or feature should you employ for this purpose?

A. Azure Data Lake Storage Gen2

B. Azure NetApp Files

C. Azure Data Share

D. Azure Table storage

29) DRAG DROP:

You have an on-premises application named App1 that customers use to manage digital images. As part of the migration to Azure, you need to recommend a data storage solution for App1 that meets specific image storage requirements and customer account requirements. The solution must:

Image Storage Requirements:

     · **Encrypt images at rest.**
     · **Allow files up to 50 MB.**

· Manage access to the images using Azure Web Application Firewall (WAF) on Azure Front Door.

Customer Account Requirements:

· Support automatic scale-out of the storage.
· Maintain the availability of App1 if a datacenter fails.
· Support reading and writing data from multiple Azure regions.

Choose the appropriate services to the correct type of data. Each service may be used once, more than once, or not at all.

Services:

a. Azure Blob Storage

b. Azure Cosmos DB

c. Azure SQL Database

d. Azure Table Storage

Answer area:

1) Image storage: ....

2) Costumer accounts: ....

30) You are in the process of designing an application responsible for aggregating content for users.

The requirement is to recommend a database solution for this application that adheres to the following criteria:

· Support SQL commands.
· Support multi-master writes.
· Guarantee low-latency read operations.

What would be your recommendation for the database

solution?

A. Azure Cosmos DB for NoSQL

B. Azure SQL Database that uses active geo-replication

C. Azure SQL Database Hyperscale

D. Azure Cosmos DB for PostgreSQL

31) You are in the process of planning the migration of on-premises MySQL databases to Azure Database for MySQL Flexible Server.

The recommendation for the Azure Database for MySQL Flexible Server configuration must align with the following requirements:

- Ensure accessibility to databases in the event of a datacenter failure.
- Minimize costs.

What compute tier should be recommended in this scenario?

A. Burstable

B. General Purpose

C. Memory Optimized

32) You are in the process of designing an application that will utilize Azure Cosmos DB to aggregate sales data from various countries. The recommendation for the app's API must align with the following requirements:

- **Support SQL queries.**
- **Support geo-replication.**
- **Enable storage and access of data relationally.**

What API should be recommended to fulfill these requirements?

A. Apache Cassandra

B. PostgreSQL

C. MongoDB

D. NoSQL

33) HOTSPOT:

You have an application generating 50,000 events per day. Your strategy involves streaming these events to an Azure Event Hub and utilizing Event Hubs Capture for implementing the cold path processing of these events. The resulting output from Event Hubs Capture will be consumed by a reporting system.

To support Event Hubs Capture, you must identify the type of Azure storage that needs to be provisioned. Additionally, you need to determine the inbound data format that the reporting system must support.

Select the appropriate options in the answer area.

Answer area:

1) Storage type:

 a. Azure Data Lake Storage Gen2

b. Premium block blobs

c. Premium file shares

2) Data format:

a. Apache Parquet

b. Avro

c. JSON

34) You have the resources shown in the following table.

Name	Type
AS1	Azure Synapse Analytics instance
CDB1	Azure Cosmos DB for NoSQL account

CDB1 hosts a container that stores continuously updated operational data.

You are designing a solution that will use AS1 to analyze the operational data daily.

You need to recommend a solution to analyze the data without affecting the performance of the operational data store.

What should you include in the recommendation?

A. Azure Data Factory with Azure Cosmos DB and Azure Synapse Analytics connectors

B. Azure Synapse Analytics with PolyBase data loading

C. Azure Synapse Link for Azure Cosmos DB

D. Azure Cosmos DB change feed

35) HOTSPOT:

You have an Azure subscription with an Azure SQL managed instance storing employee details, including social security numbers and phone numbers. To fulfill the requirements:

· The helpdesk team should only have visibility to the

last four digits of an employee's phone number.
· Cloud administrators must be restricted from accessing employee social security numbers.

Specify the necessary configurations for each column in the managed instance by selecting the appropriate options in the answer area.

Answer area:

1) Phone numbers:

a. Always Encrypted

b. Column encryption

c. Dynamic data masking

d. Transparent Data Encryption (TDE)

2) Social Security Numbers:

 a. Always Encrypted

b. Column encryption

c. Dynamic data masking

d. Transparent Data Encryption (TDE)

36) You are tasked with recommending a solution for an Azure Storage account to store data assets, ensuring it meets the following criteria:

· Supports immutable storage.
· Disables anonymous access to the storage account.
· Supports Azure Active Directory (Azure AD) permissions based on access control lists (ACL).

Provide a recommendation that addresses these requirements.

A. Azure Files

B. Azure Data Lake Storage

C. Azure NetApp Files

D. Azure Blob Storage

37) You are tasked with designing a storage solution for ingesting, storing, and analyzing petabytes of structured, semi-structured, and unstructured text data. The analyzed data will be offloaded to Azure Data Lake Storage Gen2 for long-term retention.

Your recommendation must meet the following criteria:

> • **Store the processed data.**
> • **Enable interactive analytics.**
> • **Support manual scaling, built-in autoscaling, and custom autoscaling.**

Specify the components or features that should be included in your recommendation by selecting the appropriate options in the answer area.

Answer area:

1) For storage and interactive analytics:

a. Azure Data Explorer

b. Azure Data Lake Analytics

c. Log Analytics

2) Query language:

a. KQL

B. Transact-SQL

C. U-SQL

38) HOTSPOT:

You are preparing to utilize Azure SQL as a database platform and are tasked with recommending an Azure SQL product and service tier. The recommendation should align with the following requirements:

- **Automatically adjusts compute resources in response to workload demands.**
- **Offers per-second billing.**

Specify the appropriate options in the answer area to address these requirements.

Answer area:

1) Azure SQL product:

 a. A Single Azure SQL database

 b. An Azure SQL Database elastic pool

 c. Azure SQL Managed Instance

2) Service tier:

a. Basic

b. Business Critical

c. General Purpose

d. Hyperscale

e. Standard

39) HOTSPOT:

You possess an Azure subscription and aim to implement a

solution allowing point-in-time restore for blobs in storage accounts featuring blob versioning and blob soft delete.

To achieve this, identify the type of blob to create and specify the necessary configurations for the storage accounts.

Specify the appropriate options in the answer area to address these requirements.

Answer area:

1) Blob type:

a. Append

b. Block

c. Page

2) Enable:

a. A stored access policy

b. Immutable blob storage

c. Object replication

d. The change feed

40) HOTSPOT:

Contoso, Ltd. owns an Azure subscription with the following resources:

- An Azure Synapse Analytics workspace named contosoworkspace1
- An Azure Data Lake Storage account named contosolake1
- An Azure SQL database named contososql1

Contoso's product data is transferred from contososql1 to contosolake1.

Contoso is partnered with Fabrikam Inc., which possesses an Azure subscription featuring the following resources:

- A virtual machine named FabrikamVM1 running Microsoft SQL Server 2019
- An Azure Storage account named fabrikamsa1

Contoso intends to transfer research data from FabrikamVM1 to contosolake1. Throughout the upload process, the research data will undergo transformation to align with Contoso's data formats.

The data in contosolake1 will be analyzed by using contosoworkspace1.

You need to recommend a solution that meets the following requirements:

• Upload and transform the FabrikamVM1 research data.

• Provide Fabrikam with restricted access to snapshots of the data in contosoworkspace1.

What should you recommend for each requirement?

To answer, select the appropriate options in the answer area.

Answer area:

1) Upload and transform the data:

 a. Azure Data Box Gateway

b. Azure Data Share

c. Azure Synapse pipelines

2) Provide Restricted access:

a. Azure Data Box Gateway

b. Azure Data Share

c. Azure Synapse pipelines

41) HOTSPOT:

To implement a data pipeline for integrating large amounts of data from multiple on-premises Microsoft SQL Server databases into an Azure analytics platform, consider the following actions:

- Periodically export database updates to a staging area in Azure Blob storage.
- Cleanse and transform data using a highly parallelized load process.
- Load the transformed data into a data warehouse.
- Use each batch of updates to refresh an Online Analytical Processing (OLAP) model in a managed serving layer.
- Allow thousands of end users to access the managed serving layer.

Select the appropriate options in the answer area to implement the data warehouse and serving layers.

Answer area:

1) To implement the data warehouse:

a. An Apache Spark pool in Azure Synapse Analytics

b. An Azure Synapse Analytics dedicated SQL pool

c. Azure Data Lake Analytics

2) To implement the serving layer:

a. Azure Analysis Services

b. An Apache Spark pool in Azure Synapse Analytics

c. An Azure Synapse Analytics dedicated SQL pool

42) HOTSPOT:

To deploy a relational database in Azure that meets specific requirements:

- **Support multiple read-only replicas.**
- **Automatically load balance read-only requests across all the read-only replicas.**
- **Minimize administrative effort.**

Choose the appropriate options in the answer area.

Answer area:

1) Service:

 a. A single Azure SQL database

 b. An Azure SQL Database elastic pool

 c. Azure SQL Managed Instances

2) Service tier:

a. Business Critical

b. Hyperscale

c. Premium

43) You have an application named App1 utilizing an Azure Blob Storage container named app1data. App1 uploads a cumulative transaction log file named File1.txt to a block blob in app1data every hour. File1.txt retains transaction data from the current day only.

To ensure that the last uploaded version of File1.txt can be restored from any day within a 30-day timeframe after the file

was overwritten, the solution must optimize storage space.

Specify the elements that should be incorporated into the solution while minimizing storage space.

A. container soft delete

B. blob snapshots

C. blob soft delete

D. blob versioning

44) You have 12 on-premises data sources, including Microsoft SQL Server, MySQL, and Oracle databases, containing customer information. Within your Azure subscription, you intend to establish an Azure Data Lake Storage account to centralize customer information for analysis and reporting purposes.

You are tasked with recommending a solution for automating the extraction, transformation, and loading (ETL) process to seamlessly copy new data from the on-premises data sources to the Azure Data Lake Storage account. The solution should be designed to minimize administrative effort.

What elements should be incorporated into your recommendation to achieve these objectives?

A. Azure Data Factory

B. Azure Data Explorer

C. Azure Data Share

D. Azure Data Studio

45) You have SQL Server deployed on an Azure virtual

machine, and the databases are updated nightly as part of a batch process.

You are tasked with recommending a disaster recovery solution for the data, with the following requirements:

- Ensure the ability to recover in the event of a regional outage.
- Achieve a recovery time objective (RTO) of 15 minutes.
- Meet a recovery point objective (RPO) of 24 hours.
- Support automated recovery.
- Minimize costs.

What elements should be incorporated into your recommendation to fulfill these criteria?

A. Azure virtual machine availability sets

B. Azure Disk Backup

C. an Always On availability group

D. Azure Site Recovery

46) HOTSPOT
You plan to deploy the backup policy shown in the following exhibit.

Policy 1

☷☷ Associated items　🗑 Delete　🖫 Save　✕ Discard

Backup schedule

*Frequency　　　*Time　　　　*Timezone

| Daily ⌄ | 6:00 PM ⌄ | (UTC) Coordinated Univer... ⌄ |

Instant Restore ⓘ

Retain instant recovery snapshot(s) for

| 3 ✓ | Day(s) ⓘ

Retention range

☑ Retention of daily backup point.

*At　　　　　　For

| 6:00 PM ⌄ | 90 ✓ | Day(s)

☑ Retention of weekly backup point.

*On　　　　*At　　　　For

| Sunday ⌄ | 6:00 PM ⌄ | 26 ✓ | Week(s)

☑ Retention of monthly backup point.

(**Week Based**　　Day Based)

*On　　　　*Day　　　*At　　　　For

| First ⌄ | Sunday ⌄ | 6:00 PM ⌄ | 36 | Month(s)

☐ Retention of yearly backup point.

Not Configured

Choose the answer choice that completes each statement based on the information presented in the graphic.

Hot Area:

Answer area:

1) Virtual machines that are backed up by using the policy can be recovered for up to a maximum of [answer choice]

a. 90 days

b. 26 weeks

c. 36 months

 d. 45 months

2) The minimum Recovery Point Objective (RPO) for Virtual machines that are backed up by using the policy is [answer choice]

a. 1 hour

b. 1 day

c. 1 week

d. 1 month

e. 1 year

47) You are tasked with deploying resources to host a stateless web app in an Azure subscription. The solution must satisfy the following criteria:

- **Provide access to the full .NET framework.**
- **Ensure redundancy in case of an Azure region failure.**
- **Enable administrators to access the operating system for installing custom application dependencies.**

Your proposed solution involves deploying two Azure virtual machines in two Azure regions and creating an Azure Traffic Manager profile.

Does this solution align with the specified goal?

A. Yes

B. No

48) You are tasked with deploying resources to host a stateless web app in an Azure subscription with the following requirements:

- Provide access to the full .NET framework.
- Ensure redundancy in case of an Azure region failure.
- Grant administrators access to the operating system to install custom application dependencies.

Your proposed solution involves deploying two Azure virtual machines to two Azure regions and deploying an Azure Application Gateway.

Does this solution align with the specified goal?

A. Yes

B. No

49) HOTSPOT:

You are preparing to establish an Azure Storage account to host file shares, with the intention of accessing these shares from on-premises applications that involve frequent transactions.

You need to recommend a solution to minimize latency when accessing the file shares. The solution must provide the

highest-level of resiliency for the selected storage tier.

What should you include in the recommendation?

Hot area:

Answer area:

1) Storage tier:

a. Hot

b. Premium

c. Transaction optimized

2) Redundancy:

a. Geo-redundant storage (GRS)

b. Zone-redundant storage (ZRS)

c. Locally-redundant storage (LRS)

50) You are tasked with deploying resources to host a stateless web app in an Azure subscription, and the solution must satisfy the following requirements:

- **Provide access to the full .NET framework.**
- **Ensure redundancy in case of an Azure region failure.**
- **Grant administrators access to the operating system for installing custom application dependencies.**
- **Your proposed solution involves deploying an Azure virtual machine scale set that utilizes autoscaling.**

Does this solution align with the specified goal?

A. Yes

B. No

51) HOTSPOT:

You are tasked with recommending an Azure Storage account configuration for two applications named Application1 and Application2. The configuration must adhere to the following requirements:

- **Storage for Application1 should deliver the highest transaction rates and the lowest latency possible.**
- **Storage for Application2 should offer the lowest storage costs per GB.**
- **Storage for both applications must remain available in the event of a datacenter failure.**
- **Storage for both applications should be optimized for efficient uploads and downloads.**

What options should be included in your recommendation?

Choose the appropriate selections in the answer area.

Answer area:

1) Application1:

a. BlobStorage with Standard performance, Hot access tier, and Read- access geo-redundant storage (RA-GRS) replication.

b. BlockBlobStorage with Premium performance and Zone-redundant storage (ZRS) replication.

c. General purpose v1 with Premium performance and Locally-redundant storage (LRS) replication.

d. General purpose v2 with Standard performance, Hot access tier, and Locally-redundant storage (LRS) replication.

Application2:

a. BlobStorage with Standard performance, Hot access tier, and Read- access geo-redundant storage (RA-GRS) replication.

b. BlockBlobStorage with Premium performance and Zone-redundant storage (ZRS) replication.

c. General purpose v1 with Premium performance and Locally-redundant storage (LRS) replication.

d. General purpose v2 with Standard performance, Hot access tier, and Locally-redundant storage (LRS) replication.

52) HOTSPOT:

You are preparing to develop a new app that will store business-critical data, and the app must satisfy the following requirements:

- **Prevent new data from being modified for one year.**
- **Maximize data resiliency.**
- **Minimize read latency.**

What storage solution should you recommend for the app?

Choose the appropriate options in the answer area.

Answer area:

1) Storage account type:

a. Premium block blobs

b. Standard general-purpose v1

c. Standard general-purpose v2

2) Redundancy:

a. Zone-redundant storage (ZRS)

b. Locally-redundant storage (LRS)

53) To deploy 10 applications on Azure, utilize two Azure

Kubernetes Service (AKS) clusters, each deployed in distinct Azure regions. The deployment must adhere to the following specifications:

Guarantee uninterrupted availability of applications in the event of a single AKS cluster failure.

Enable SSL encryption for internet-bound traffic without the need for individual SSL configuration on each container.

Which service should you include in the recommendation?

A. Azure Front Door

B. Azure Traffic Manager

C. AKS ingress controller

D. Azure Load Balancer

54) HOTSPOT:

You have an on-premises file server that stores 2 TB of data files.

You plan to move the data files to Azure Blob Storage in the West Europe Azure region.

You need to recommend a storage account type to store the data files and a replication solution for the storage account. The solution must meet the following requirements:

- Be available if a single Azure datacenter fails.
- Support storage tiers.
- Minimize cost.

What should you recommend? To answer, select the appropriate options in the answer area.

Hot area:

Answer area:

1) Storage account type:

a. Premium block blobs

b. Standard General-purpose v1

c. Standard General-purpose v2

2) Redundancy:

a. Geo-redundant storage (GRS)

b. Zone-redundant storage (ZRS)

c. Locally-redundant storage (LRS)

d. Read-access geo-redundant storage (RA-GRS)

55) You have an Azure web app named App1 and an Azure key vault named KV1.

App1 stores database connection strings in KV1.

App1 performs the following types of requests to KV1:

∞ **Get**

∞ **List**

∞ **Wrap**

∞ **Delete**

Unwrap:

∞ **Backup**

∞ **Decrypt**

∞ **Encrypt**

You are evaluating the continuity of service for App1.

You need to identify the following if the Azure region that hosts KV1 becomes unavailable:

∞ To where will KV1 fail over?

∞ During the failover, which request type will be unavailable?

What should you identify?

To answer, choose the appropriate options in the answer area.

Hot area:

Answer area:

1) To where will KV1 fail over:

a. A server in the same availability set

b. A server in the same fault domain

c. A server in the paired region

d. A virtual machine in a scale set

2) During the failover, which request type will be unavailable:

a. Get

b. List

c. Wrap

d. Delete

e. Unwrap

f. Backup

g. Decrypt

h. Encrypt

56) DRAG DROP:

Your company identifies the following business continuity and disaster recovery objectives for virtual machines that host sales, finance, and reporting applications in the company's on-premises data center:

∞ The sales application must be able to fail over to a second on-premises data center.

∞ The reporting application must be able to recover point-in-time data at a daily granularity. The RTO is eight hours.

∞ The finance application requires that data be retained for seven years. In the event of a disaster, the application must be able to run from Azure. The recovery time objective (RTO) is 10 minutes.

You need to recommend which services meet the business continuity and disaster recovery objectives. The solution must minimize costs.

What should you recommend for each application?

To answer, choose the appropriate services to the correct applications.

Each service may be used once, more than once, or not at all.

Select and Place:

Services:

a. Azure Backup only

b. Azure Site Recovery and Azure Backup

c. Azure Site Recovery only

Answer area:

1) Sales: ....

2) Finance: ....

3) Reporting: ....

57) Design a resilient Azure SQL database with the following requirements:

- **Enable failover between replicas without experiencing data loss.**
- **Ensure the database remains accessible even in the event of a zone outage.**
- **Optimize costs for the deployment.**

Which deployment option would be most suitable for meeting these specifications?

A. Azure SQL Managed Instance Business Critical.

B. Azure SQL Database Premium.

C. Azure SQL Database Basic.

D. Azure SQL Managed Instance General Purpose.

58) You need to deploy resources to host a stateless web app in an Azure subscription. The solution must meet the following requirements:

- **Provide access to the full .NET framework.**
- **Provide redundancy if an Azure region fails.**
- **Grant administrators access to the operating system to install custom application dependencies.**

Solution: You deploy a web app in an Isolated App Service plan.

Does this meet the goal?

A. Yes

B. No

59) HOTSPOT:

You have an on-premises Microsoft SQL Server database named SQL1.

You plan to migrate SQL1 to Azure.

You need to recommend a hosting solution for SQL1. The solution must meet the following requirements:

• Support the deployment of multiple secondary, read-only replicas.

• Support automatic replication between primary and secondary replicas.

• Support failover between primary and secondary replicas within a 15-minute recovery time objective (RTO).

What should you include in the solution?

To answer, choose the appropriate options in the answer area.

Answer area:

1) Azure service or service tier:

a. Azure SQL Database

b. Azure SQL Managed Instance

c. The Hyperscale service tier

2) Replication mechanism:

a. Active Geo-replication

b. Auto-failover groups

c. Standard Geo-replication

60) HOTSPOT:

You have two on-premises Microsoft SQL Server 2017 instances that host an Always On availability group named AG1. AG1 contains a single database named DB1.

You have an Azure subscription that contains a virtual machine named VM1. VM1 runs Linux and contains a SQL Server 2019 instance.

You need to migrate DB1 to VM1. The solution must minimize downtime on DB1.

What should you do?

To answer, choose the appropriate options in the answer area.

Answer area:

1) Prepare for the migration by:

a. Adding a secondary replica to AG1

b. Creating an Always On Availability group on VM1

c. Upgrading the on-premises SQL Server instances

2) Perform the migration by using:

a. A distributed availability group

b. Azure Migrate

c. Log shipping

Notes:

....

....

....
....
....
....
....
....
....
....
....
....
....
....
....
....
....

ANSWERS AND EXPLANATION

1) AB

To efficiently monitor costs on a per-project basis across 12 Azure subscriptions with resources spanning multiple subscriptions, you should include the following components in the solution:

A. budgets

B. resource tags

Explanation:

Budgets (Option A): Creating budgets in Microsoft Cost Management allows you to set spending limits and receive alerts when thresholds are reached. This is essential for monitoring costs on a per-project basis and helps you stay within predefined budget constraints.

Resource tags (Option B): Utilizing resource tags allows you to categorize and label resources across subscriptions. By tagging resources with project-specific information, you can easily filter and organize cost data for each project within Microsoft Cost Management.

These two components, budgets, and resource tags, provide an effective way to monitor costs per project while minimizing administrative effort.

2) 1) b, 2) a

To trigger the compliance scans, use Azure CLI

Reference:

https://learn.microsoft.com/en-us/azure/governance/policy/
how-to/get-compliance-data#on-demand-evaluation-scan

An evaluation scan for a subscription or a resource group can be started with Azure CLI, Azure PowerShell, a call to the REST API, or by using the Azure Policy Compliance Scan GitHub Action. This scan is an asynchronous process. An evaluation scan for a subscription or a resource group can be started with Azure CLI, Azure PowerShell, a call to the REST API, or by using the Azure Policy Compliance Scan GitHub Action. This scan is an asynchronous process.

To generate alerts, configure diagnostic settings for the Azure activity logs.

Also, note that on-demand evaluation scan can be triggered not only by Azure CLI, but also using Azure PowerShell, REST API call and Azure Policy Compliance Scan GitHub action.

Reference:

https://learn.microsoft.com/en-us/azure/azure-monitor/alerts/
alerts-create-new-alert-rule

3) 1) a, 2) a

1. For the blobs - a user delegation SAS only

To maximize security, it's better to use a user delegation SAS:

From docs: As a security best practice, we recommend that you use Azure AD credentials, when possible, rather than the account key, which can be more easily compromised. When your application design requires shared access signatures, use Azure

AD credentials to create a user delegation SAS to help ensure better security.

This also prevents using shared keys & supports time-limited access. Note: user delegation SAS do not support stored access policies.

2. For the file shares - Azure AD credentials

It fulfills the requirement to maximize security (the most secure way recommended by Microsoft), but doesn't support time-limited access, which is optional and has lower priority than security.

Reference:

https://learn.microsoft.com/en-us/rest/api/storageservices/create-user-delegation-sas.

4)

1 - Azure Monitor Data collection

2 – KQL

To forward the logs:

b. An Azure Monitor data collection endpoint

Explanation: Azure Monitor provides data collection endpoints that allow you to forward logs to Log Analytics workspaces. These endpoints are specifically designed for receiving and processing logs from various sources, including virtual machines. Using an Azure Monitor data collection endpoint is the appropriate method for forwarding logs to a Log Analytics workspace.

To transform the logs and store the data:

a. A KQL query

Explanation: KQL (Kusto Query Language) is the language used for querying and analyzing data in Azure Monitor. It is specifically designed for querying data stored in Log Analytics workspaces. By using KQL queries, you can transform and analyze the JSON-formatted logs, and store the results in a table within the Log Analytics workspace. KQL provides powerful capabilities for data transformation and analysis in Log Analytics.

Reference:

https://learn.microsoft.com/en-us/azure/azure-monitor/agents/data-collection-rule-azure-monitor-agent)

5)

Recommendations for the provided requirements:

1. To collect the event logs:

b. Azure Lighthouse

Explanation: Azure Lighthouse provides cross-tenant management capabilities, allowing you to collect event logs from multiple Azure subscriptions across different Azure AD tenants and send them to a single Log Analytics workspace.

2. To support the use of DCRs:

b. The Azure Monitor agent

Explanation: The Azure Monitor agent is responsible for collecting and sending telemetry data, including Windows security events, to Azure Monitor services. It supports data collection rules (DCRs) to define which specific events to collect, making it suitable for meeting the specified requirement.

Reference:

https://learn.microsoft.com/en-us/azure/azure-monitor/ agents/agents-overview#install-the-agent-and-configure-data-collection

6) B

CLR is supported on SQL Managed instance and not on Azure SQL Database.

B. Azure SQL Managed Instance

Explanation:

Minimize management overhead: Azure SQL Managed Instance provides a fully managed platform-as-a-service (PaaS) solution. This means that many aspects of database management, including patching, backups, and high availability, are handled automatically by the service, reducing management overhead.

Enable user authentication using Azure AD credentials: Azure SQL Managed Instance supports Azure AD authentication, allowing users to authenticate using their Azure AD credentials. This aligns with the requirement for Azure AD authentication.

Minimize required database changes: Azure SQL Managed Instance is designed to be highly compatible with on-premises SQL Server. This compatibility reduces the changes required for migration, providing a smoother transition for databases characterized by CLR-based stored procedures.

Therefore, Azure SQL Managed Instance is the suitable choice to meet the specified requirements.

Reference:

https://learn.microsoft.com/en-us/azure/azure-sql/database/features-comparison?view=azuresql#features-of-sql-database-and-sql-managed-instance

7) BC

The two potential Azure services that can help achieve the objective of duplicating the company files from the on-premises file server (Server1) to the Azure Blob Storage account (store1) are:

B. an Azure Import/Export job:

Explanation: Azure Import/Export enables you to transfer large amounts of data to and from Azure Blob Storage using physical drives. You can ship a hard drive containing the company files to an Azure datacenter, where the data will be imported into the Azure Blob Storage account.

C. Azure Data Factory:

Explanation: Azure Data Factory allows you to create data-driven workflows to orchestrate and automate data movement and data transformation. You can use Azure Data Factory to transfer the company files from Server1 to Azure Blob Storage (store1) as part of a data pipeline.

These services provide efficient methods for transferring and duplicating large amounts of data from an on-premises server to Azure Blob Storage.

Extra explanation

A. an Azure Logic Apps integration account

No, this is an integration service with visual flows with If-Then style logic. It does not support a way to import data from on-premise to blob storage

B. an Azure Import/Export job

Agree, with other people here.

C. Azure Data Factory

Agree, is a way of importing data, but looking at 500GB it is a bit of overkill

D. an Azure Analysis services On-premises data gateway

Not a data import option

E. an Azure Batch account

Is part of Azure Batch service and involve HPC job scheduling etc. but is not a way of importing or exporting data from on-premise to Azure

Note:

For 500GB we would probably use AzCopy instead.

If it was a Typo and actually 500TB we would use Azure Data Box Heavy or maybe the Azure Import/Export Service if you provide your own drives.

Reference:

https://docs.microsoft.com/en-gb/azure/storage/blobs/storage-blobs-introduction#move-data-to-blob-storage

8) D

For ensuring that each new application can read pertinent transactions and considering the scenario described, the recommended alternative to the storage account queue is:

D. One Azure Service Bus Topic

Explanation:

Azure Service Bus Topics are suitable for scenarios where multiple applications need to receive and process messages independently. Each application can have its own subscription to the topic, allowing them to filter and process messages relevant to their specific requirements.

As more applications are anticipated in the future, Azure Service Bus Topics provide a scalable and flexible messaging solution where each application can subscribe to the pertinent messages without affecting the others.

This approach allows for better decoupling of applications and ensures that new applications can be added easily to process specific shipping requests.

Therefore, the recommended choice is D. One Azure Service Bus Topic.

No doubt, the Service Bus Topic is exactly what you would need if multiple applications want to send messages to consumers.

Reference:

https://learn.microsoft.com/en-us/training/modules/design-application-architecture/3-design-messaging-solution

9) To design a storage solution meeting the specified requirements, you should recommend the following:

1. Storage account type:

 b. BlockBlobStorage

2. Storage service:

a. Blob

Explanation:

BlockBlobStorage is optimized for scenarios with high throughput and is suitable for storing large amounts of frequently used data.

The Blob storage service is the appropriate service for storing large amounts of data. Blobs are ideal for unstructured data, such as images, videos, and documents.

The combination of BlockBlobStorage and Blob service meets the requirements of maximizing data throughput, preventing data modification for one year, and minimizing latency for read and write operations.

Therefore, the recommended options are b. BlockBlobStorage for storage account type and a. Blob for storage service.

The keyword is maximizing data throughput

BlockBlobStorage provide a very low latency(x40) (Read and Write) and Throughput (x5)

BECAUSE: One big file is splitted in "blobs" that are processed in parallel (for read and write)

Reference:

https://azure.microsoft.com/en-us/blog/premium-block-blob-storage-a-new-level-of-performance/

10)

App1: Storage1 and storage3 only

App2: Storage1 and storage4 only

Note: Storage2, StorageV2 with Premium Performance does NOT exist

GENERATION V1 ==> CANNOT HAVE LIFECYCLE

GENERATION V2 => CAN HAVE LIFECYCLE

PREMIUM FILE STORAGE ==> CANNOT HAVE LIFECYCLE

PREMIUM BLOG ==> CANNOT HAVE LIFECYCLE (FYI - I TESTED THESE). MORE OF FYI

WE'VE TESTED ALL ABOVE

THEREFORE

STANDARD ==> LIFE CYCLE YES (STORAGE 1 AND STORAGE 3)

APPS DATA - STORAGE 1 AND 4

STORAGE 2 ==> V2 PREMIUM ==> THIS SERVICE DOES NOT EXIST IN AZURE

STORAGE V1 STANDARD ONLY EXIST (WHICH IS WHY STORAGE 2 IS NEVER AN ANSWER)

Reference:

https://docs.microsoft.com/en-ca/azure/storage/common/ storage-account-overview?toc=/azure/storage/blobs/ toc.json#types-of-storage-accounts

11) C

For storing video files ranging from 50 MB to 12 GB in an Azure-hosted application that uses certificate-based authentication and is accessible to internet users, the recommended storage option considering optimal read performance and minimized storage costs is:

C. Azure Blob Storage

Explanation:

Azure Blob Storage is specifically designed for handling unstructured data, making it suitable for storing large video files.

It provides excellent read performance for streaming and downloading large files.

Azure Blob Storage is cost-effective, offering different storage tiers like Hot, Cool, and Archive to optimize costs based on data access patterns. For infrequently accessed video files, the Cool or Archive tiers can help minimize storage costs.

This option aligns well with the requirements of optimal read performance and cost efficiency for large video files.

Therefore, the recommended choice is C. Azure Blob Storage.

Azure Blob storage is Microsoft's object storage solution for the cloud. Blob storage is optimized for storing massive amounts of unstructured data, such as text or binary data.

- Blob storage is ideal for:
- Serving images or documents directly to a browser.
- Storing files for distributed access.
- Streaming video and audio.
- Storing data for backup and restore, disaster recovery, and archiving.
- Storing data for analysis by an on-premises or Azure-

hosted service.

Objects in Blob storage can be accessed from anywhere in the world via HTTP or HTTPS. Users or client applications can access blobs via URLs, the Azure Storage REST API, Azure PowerShell, Azure CLI, or an Azure Storage client library.

Reference:

https://docs.microsoft.com/en-gb/azure/storage/common/storage-introduction#blob-storage

12) A

Databases vary in usage so an elastic pool would fit best.

For a SQL database solution encompassing 20 databases, each with a size of 20 GB and diverse usage patterns, while aiming to meet specific requirements, the recommended choice is:

A. An elastic pool that contains 20 Azure SQL databases

Explanation:

Achieve a Service Level Agreement (SLA) of 99.99% uptime: Azure SQL Database provides high availability and supports SLAs with 99.99% uptime.

Dynamically scale compute resources: Azure SQL Database elastic pools allow for dynamic scaling of compute resources across multiple databases, accommodating varying usage patterns efficiently.

Incorporate reserved capacity: Elastic pools offer a cost-effective solution with the ability to reserve capacity, optimizing costs.

Minimize compute charges: Elastic pools help minimize compute charges by allowing multiple databases to share resources within a pool based on demand.

Therefore, the recommended option is A. An elastic pool that contains 20 Azure SQL databases.

Reference:

https://docs.microsoft.com/en-us/azure/azure-sql/database/elastic-pool-overview

13) 1) a, 2) d

1: Azure SQL Database -

Azure SQL Database:

Database size always depends on the underlying service tiers (e.g. Basic, Business Critical, Hyperscale).

It supports databases of up to 100 TB with Hyperscale service tier model.

Active geo-replication is a feature that lets you to create a continuously synchronized readable secondary database for a primary database. The readable secondary database may be in the same Azure region as the primary, or, more commonly, in a different region. This kind of readable secondary databases are also known as geo-secondaries, or geo-replicas.

Azure SQL Database and SQL Managed Instance enable you to dynamically add more resources to your database with minimal downtime.

2: Hyperscale -

Incorrect Answers:

⟳ SQL Server on Azure VM: geo-replication not supported.

∞ Azure Synapse Analytics is not optimized for online transaction processing (OLTP).

∞ Azure SQL Managed Instance max database size is up to currently available instance size (depending on the number of vCores).

Max instance storage size (reserved) - 2 TB for 4 vCores

- 8 TB for 8 vCores

- 16 TB for other sizes

Support scaling up and down: The Hyperscale service tier supports scaling compute resources up and down based on your workload requirements.

Support geo-redundant backups: It offers automatic backups with the ability to enable geo-redundant backups to ensure data durability in case of regional disasters.

Support a database of up to 75 TB: Hyperscale supports databases up to 100 TB in size, which meets the requirement of 75 TB.

Be optimized for online transaction processing (OLTP): Azure SQL Database Hyperscale is designed to handle OLTP workloads with high performance and low latency.

In summary, you should include Azure SQL Database with the Hyperscale service tier in your database architecture design to meet all the listed requirements.

Azure SQL Database with Hyperscale (support up to 100TB).

https://docs.microsoft.com/en-us/azure/azure-sql/database/service-tier-hyperscale#:~:text=A%20Hyperscale%20database%20is%20created%20with%20a%20starting,about%20Hyperscale%20pricing%2C%20see%20Azure%20SQL

%20Database%20Pricing

Managed Instance is incorrect because the database limit is 2-8TB max.

https://docs.microsoft.com/en-us/azure/azure-sql/managed-instance/resource-limits#:~:text=Up%20to%20280%2C %20unless%20the%20instance%20storage%20size,TB %29%20and%20Azure%20Premium%20Disk%20storage %20allocation%20space.

14) CD

For the scenario described, the two recommended services are:

C. Azure Cosmos DB SQL API

D. Azure Time Series Insights

Explanation:

C. Azure Cosmos DB SQL API:

Azure Cosmos DB is a globally distributed, multi-model database service that supports various data models, including document, graph, and key-value. The SQL API allows you to interact with Cosmos DB using a SQL-like query language. This service is suitable for handling large volumes of IoT data with its scalable and globally distributed nature. It can easily accommodate the high ingestion rate of 50,000 records per second, making it suitable for real-time data processing and analytics.

D. Azure Time Series Insights:

Azure Time Series Insights is designed specifically for handling time-series data, which is common in IoT scenarios where data is generated over time. It provides an optimized storage and query engine for time-series data and supports quick visualization and analysis of historical and real-time data. Given that the IoT devices are streaming data that includes time information, Azure Time Series Insights is well-suited for efficiently storing, querying, and visualizing this type of data.

Therefore, using Azure Cosmos DB SQL API for general data storage and Azure Time Series Insights for time-series data would provide a comprehensive solution for storing and querying the IoT data in near real time.

Need to find a service to store and query the data.

A. Azure Table Storage: You can't query data.

B. Azure Event Grid: You can't store or query data.

C. Azure Cosmos DB SQL API: You can store and query data.

D. Azure Time Series Insights: You can store and query data.

Cosmos dB SQL API is somewhat confusing as an accurate answer though:

https://docs.microsoft.com/en-gb/azure/cosmos-db/use-cases#iot-and-telematics

15) A

The recommended solution that meets the specified criteria for supporting SQL commands, multi-master writes, and guaranteeing low latency for read operations is:

A. Azure Cosmos DB SQL API

Explanation:

Support SQL commands:

Azure Cosmos DB with the SQL API supports SQL-like query

language for querying and interacting with data.

Support multi-master writes:

Azure Cosmos DB provides multi-master capabilities, allowing writes to be performed on any region and having the changes propagate across all regions.

Guarantee low latency for read operations:

Azure Cosmos DB offers low-latency read operations globally due to its multi-region, multi-master architecture. Users can read data from the nearest region, minimizing latency.

Option B (Azure SQL Database with active geo-replication) provides multi-region redundancy but might not offer the same global distribution and low-latency read capabilities as Azure Cosmos DB.

Option C (Azure SQL Database Hyperscale) is designed for large-scale OLTP workloads but may not provide the same global distribution and low-latency read capabilities as Azure Cosmos DB.

Option D (Azure Database for PostgreSQL) is a relational database service for PostgreSQL and might not offer the same level of global distribution and multi-master writes as Azure Cosmos DB.

Therefore, Azure Cosmos DB with the SQL API is the most suitable choice for meeting all the specified requirements.

https://learn.microsoft.com/en-us/azure/cosmos-db/introduction#key-benefits

- Gain unparalleled SLA-backed speed and throughput, fast global access, and instant elasticity. Real-time access with fast read and write latencies globally, and throughput and consistency all backed by SLAs

- Multi-region writes and data distribution to any Azure region with just a button.

With Cosmos DB's novel multi-region (multi-master) writes replication protocol, every region supports both writes and reads. The multi-region writes capability also enables:

Unlimited elastic writes and read scalability.

99.999% read and write availability all around the world.

Guaranteed reads and writes served in less than 10 milliseconds at the 99th percentile.

Reference:

https://docs.microsoft.com/en-us/azure/cosmos-db/distribute-data-globally

16) Yes, No, No

1: Yes: Auditing works fine for a Standard account.

2: No: Auditing limitations: Premium storage is currently not supported.

3: No: Auditing limitations: Premium storage is currently not supported.

Concept to remember

1. To write into storage, it must be in the same region.

2. To write in log analytics space – can be in different region.

Since we're using concept 1, we can only write into the same region. It has nothing to do with pricing tier.

Auditing limitations

Premium storage is currently not supported.

https://docs.microsoft.com/en-us/azure/azure-sql/database/auditing-overview

https://docs.microsoft.com/en-us/azure/azure-sql/database/auditing-overview#auditing-limitations

17) 1) d, 2) b

1. From the SQL server 2012 database to Azure SQL Database:

d. Data Migration Assistant.

The Data Migration Assistant (DMA) helps you upgrade to a modern data platform by detecting compatibility issues that can impact database functionality in your new version of SQL Server or Azure SQL Database. DMA recommends performance and reliability improvements for your target environment and allows you to move your schema, data, and uncontained objects from your source server to your target server.

2. From the table in the SQL server 2014 database to Azure Cosmos DB:

b. Azure Cosmos DB Data Migration tool.

The Azure Cosmos DB Data Migration tool is an open-source solution that imports data to Azure Cosmos DB from a variety of sources, including SQL Server. For the SQL API, the tool supports import from JSON files, MongoDB, SQL Server, CSV files, Azure Table storage, Amazon DynamoDB, and other Azure Cosmos DB databases.

Azure Cosmos DB Data Migration Tool can used to migrate a SQL

Server Database table to Azure Cosmos.

Incorrect:

AzCopy is a command-line utility that you can use to copy blobs or files to or from a storage account.

Reference:

1.   https://docs.microsoft.com/en-us/azure/azure-sql/migration-guides/database/sql-server-to-sql-database-overview?view=azuresql

Data migration services

2.   https://docs.microsoft.com/en-us/azure/cosmos-db/cosmosdb-migrationchoices

18) D

For automating the monthly transfer of web access logs from Azure Blob Storage to Azure SQL Database, the recommended option is:

D. Azure Data Factory

Explanation:

Azure Data Factory is a cloud-based data integration service designed for orchestrating and automating data workflows. In this scenario, you can use Azure Data Factory to create a pipeline that moves data from Azure Blob Storage to Azure SQL Database on a monthly schedule, facilitating the generation of reports from the access logs.

The other options are not well-suited for this particular use case:

A. Microsoft SQL Server Migration Assistant (SSMA): SSMA is generally used for migrating databases to SQL Server and is not designed for regular, automated data transfers.

B. Data Migration Assistant (DMA): DMA is used for assessing and migrating on-premises databases to Azure SQL Database but is not intended for recurrent data upload tasks.

C. AzCopy: AzCopy is a command-line tool for copying data to and from Azure Storage. While it is useful for bulk data transfers, it lacks the scheduling and workflow orchestration features needed for automated monthly uploads.

Therefore, Azure Data Factory is the appropriate recommendation for automating the monthly data transfer from Azure Blob Storage to Azure SQL Database.

You should recommend using Azure Data Factory for this scenario. Azure Data Factory is a cloud-based data integration service that allows you to create, schedule, and manage data pipelines. In this case, you can create a pipeline to automatically extract data from the Azure Blob Storage, transform the data if needed, and load it into the Azure SQL Database on a monthly basis. This will help you generate the required monthly reports from the access logs.

Reference:

https://docs.microsoft.com/en-us/azure/data-factory/tutorial-copy-data-tool

19) AD

Since the archive tier is the cheapest for storing data.

In addition, a maximum of 15 hours may be required to rehydrate the data from an archive tier; the requirements are met.

The available access tiers include:

- Hot: Optimized for storing data that is accessed frequently.

- Cool: Optimized for storing data that is infrequently accessed and stored for at least 30 days.

- Archive: Optimized for storing data that is rarely accessed and stored for at least 180 days with flexible latency requirements (on the order of hours).

Since the files are accessed rarely and you need to minimize storage costs, the Archive tier is appropriate. Both A and D suggest setting the files to the Archive access tier.

Please note that Archive tier data is offline and it takes time to rehydrate data to an online tier if/when access is needed, but it satisfies your requirement of the files being available within 24 hours of being requested. In addition, creating an Azure Blob Storage or general-purpose v2 storage account allows you to utilize these access tiers, as they are not available in the general-purpose v1 accounts.

https://docs.microsoft.com/en-us/azure/storage/blobs/access-tiers-overview

While a blob is in the Archive tier, it can't be read or modified. To read or download a blob in the Archive tier, you must first rehydrate it to an online tier, either Hot or Cool. Data in the Archive tier can take up to 15 hours to rehydrate, depending on the priority you specify for the rehydration operation. For more information about blob rehydration, see Overview of blob rehydration from the Archive tier.

20) B

B. two databases on the same Azure SQL managed instance

An Azure SQL Managed Instance is a fully managed SQL Server Database Engine hosted in Azure that provides most of the SQL Server capabilities. It supports features like cross-database queries and transactions, which is crucial for your requirement of supporting server-side transactions across DB1 and DB2. Additionally, since it's a fully managed solution, it minimizes the administrative effort needed to update and maintain the system.

https://docs.microsoft.com/en-us/azure/azure-sql/database/elastic-transactions-overview?view=azuresql

A server-side distributed transactions using Transact-SQL are available only for Azure SQL Managed Instance. Distributed transaction can be executed only between Managed Instances that belong to the same Server trust group. In this scenario, Managed Instances need to use linked server to reference each other.

Extra explanation:

Azure SQL Managed Instance (Option B): This option allows both DB1 and DB2 to be hosted on the same managed instance. Azure SQL Managed Instance provides a fully managed SQL Server instance with compatibility benefits, and it supports distributed transactions. This means you can perform server-side transactions that span multiple databases on the same managed instance.

The other options have limitations or do not meet all the specified requirements:

Two Azure SQL databases in an elastic pool (Option A): While elastic pools are useful for managing and scaling multiple databases, they do not support distributed transactions across databases.

Two databases on the same SQL Server instance on an Azure virtual machine (Option C): This option involves more management overhead as compared to Azure SQL Managed Instance. Additionally, managing updates and maintenance may require more effort.

Two Azure SQL databases on different Azure SQL Database servers (Option D): Distributed transactions across servers may introduce complexity and may not be the most efficient way to handle server-side transactions.

Therefore, Option B (two databases on the same Azure SQL managed instance) is the recommended solution for hosting DB1 and DB2 in Azure while meeting the specified criteria.

21) B

B. Azure SQL Database Premium

To meet the requirements of a highly available Azure SQL database with no data loss during failover and availability during a zone outage, you should use Azure SQL Database Premium. The Premium tier provides built-in support for active geo-replication, which allows you to create readable secondary replicas in different regions, ensuring the database remains available in the event of a zone outage. Additionally, the Premium tier offers better performance and more resources compared to the Basic and General-Purpose tiers, while Hyperscale, although highly scalable, can be more costly than the Premium tier.

Note: Zone-redundant configuration is not available in SQL Managed Instance. In SQL Database this feature is only available when the Gen5 hardware is selected.

Incorrect:

Not A: Hyperscale is more expensive than Premium.

Not C: Need Premium for Availability Zones.

Not D: Zone redundant configuration that is free on Azure SQL Premium is not available on Azure SQL Managed Instance.

https://learn.microsoft.com/en-us/azure/azure-sql/database/sql-database-paas-overview?view=azuresql#service-tiers

The Premium service tier is designed for OLTP applications with high transaction rates and low latency I/O requirements. It offers the highest resilience to failures by using several isolated replicas.

22) 1) c, 2) b

1. Storage Account type:

c. GP v2 Hot.

Considering the data will be accessed daily, the Hot access tier is the most cost-effective for storing frequently accessed data.

2. Configuration to prevent the modification and deletions:

b. Container access policy.

The Container access policy is indeed the place to configure Azure's Immutable Blob Storage to ensure data is retained without modifications or deletions for a specified amount of time, which suits your needs. The Azure Blob Storage's Immutable Blob Storage feature provides a WORM (Write Once, Read Many) capability which aligns with your requirements perfectly.

Answer is GPv2 HOT to have frequent access:

https://docs.microsoft.com/en-us/azure/storage/blobs/access-tiers-overview

Answer is container access (immutable) policy at least at the container scope.

https://docs.microsoft.com/en-us/azure/storage/blobs/immutable-storage-overview

You set the resources lock as read-only and delete prevention but can to for data, that is only for resources change not for in the data.

23) 1) b, 2) c

1. Data store for the ingestion data:

b. Azure Data Lake Storage Gen2.

Azure Data Lake Storage Gen2 is designed for big data analytics, it combines the power of a high-performance file system with massive scale and economy to help you speed up your big data analytics. It allows the data to be organized in directories by date and time.

2. Data store for the data warehouse:

c. Azure SQL Database Hyperscale.

Azure SQL Database Hyperscale is a highly scalable service tier that is designed to provide high performance, and supports up to 100 TB of data. The Hyperscale service tier in Azure SQL Database is the newest service tier in the vCorebased purchasing model. This service tier is a highly scalable storage and compute performance tier that leverages the Azure architecture to scale out the storage and compute resources for an Azure SQL Database substantially beyond the limits available for the General Purpose and Business Critical service tiers.

Reference:

https://learn.microsoft.com/en-us/azure/azure-sql/database/service-tier-hyperscale?view=azuresql#what-are-the-hyperscale-capabilities

24) A

A. RSA 3072

RSA 3072 provides a higher level of encryption strength compared to RSA 2048. While RSA 4096 offers even stronger encryption, it is not supported by Azure SQL Database and Azure SQL Managed Instance for TDE protectors.

By choosing RSA 3072 for the TDE protector, you ensure strong encryption for your Azure SQL Managed Instance while complying with the platform's requirements. This will help protect sensitive data and maintain compliance with relevant security standards and regulations.

Reference:

https://learn.microsoft.com/en-us/azure/azure-sql/database/transparent-data-encryption-tde-overview?view=azuresql&tabs=azure-portal

25) CD

To meet the requirements of storing and querying data from

50,000 IoT devices streaming data at a high rate, with the need for near real-time visualization, the two recommended services are:

C. Azure Cosmos DB for NoSQL

D. Azure Time Series Insights

Explanation:

Azure Cosmos DB for NoSQL (Option C): Azure Cosmos DB is a globally distributed, multi-model database service that supports various data models, including document, graph, and key-value. It is well-suited for handling large volumes of IoT data with its scalable and globally distributed nature. It can handle the high ingestion rate of 50,000 records per second. The NoSQL data model is flexible and can accommodate the variety of data from IoT devices.

Azure Time Series Insights (Option D): Azure Time Series Insights is specifically designed for handling time-series data, which is common in IoT scenarios where data is generated over time. It provides an optimized storage and query engine for time-series data, allowing for efficient querying and visualization of historical and real-time data.

Options A (Azure Table Storage) and B (Azure Event Grid) may not be as well-suited for the specific requirements of high-volume, time-series IoT data and near real-time visualization.

Therefore, the comprehensive solution for storing and querying data from 50,000 IoT devices in near real time would involve using Azure Cosmos DB for NoSQL and Azure Time Series Insights.

Real-time access with fast read and write latencies globally, and throughput and consistency all backed by SLAs https://learn.microsoft.com/en-us/azure/cosmos-db/introduction

Azure Time Series Insights is a fully managed analytics, storage, and visualization service that makes it simple to explore and analyze billions of IoT events simultaneously.

https://learn.microsoft.com/en-us/azure/time-series-insights/time-series-insights-explorer

26) 1) c, 2) b

1. Storage account type:

c. General purpose v2 with hot access tier for blobs

The hot access tier provides lower data access costs compared to the cool access tier, making it more suitable for minimizing charges when data is accessed daily. Although the cool tier has lower storage costs, the data access charges are higher, which would not be ideal for your scenario. Premium block blobs are meant for high-performance scenarios and are not necessary for a small dataset of less than 10 GB.

2. Configuration to prevent modifications and deletions:

b. Container access policy

You can create a container access policy with specific permissions (in this case, read-only) and set an expiry time of five years. This policy prevents modifications and deletions, while still allowing the data to be read. After five years, the policy will expire, and the data can be deleted but not modified. Storage account resource locks and container access level settings don't offer the same granularity of control over the data as the container access policy.

Note: It's not the same as the question 22. This question has a different option (Premium Block blobs) and this is the correct answer, because access cost to Premium Block is cheaper than GPv2 hot tier.

Reference:

https://azure.microsoft.com/en-us/pricing/details/storage/blobs/

27) 1) a, 2) b

Can query delta lake with Serverless SQL pool but won't be able to update it.

- Only Apache Spark pools support updates to Delta Lakes files. It can also be used to query long-time series as well

Serverless SQL pool doesn't provides updates:

https://learn.microsoft.com/en-us/azure/synapse-analytics/sql/query-delta-lake-format.

Updates are possible in Apache Spark: https://docs.delta.io/latest/delta-update.html

Apache Spark can be also used for small scenarios as it's not that expensive and is often used by data engineers, not just big data engineers.

Hash-distributed tables are used for VERY LARGE FACT TABLES.

As per documentation:

https://learn.microsoft.com/en-us/azure/synapse-analytics/sql-data-warehouse/sql-data-warehouse-tables-distribute

Consider using a hash-distributed table when:

The table size on disk is more than 2 GB.

28) A

For migrating an on-premises storage solution to Azure with a requirement to support the Hadoop Distributed File System (HDFS), the recommended option is:

A. Azure Data Lake Storage Gen2

Explanation:

Azure Data Lake Storage Gen2 (Option A): It is designed for big data analytics and supports Hadoop Distributed File System (HDFS). It provides capabilities for storing and analyzing large amounts of data with features like hierarchical namespace and fine-grained access control. This makes it suitable for scenarios involving big data workloads, including those using Hadoop.

Options B, C, and D are not specifically designed to support Hadoop Distributed File System:

Azure NetApp Files (Option B): It is a fully managed file service, but it may not be the most suitable for HDFS-based workloads.

Azure Data Share (Option C): It is designed for sharing data between organizations but does not provide the HDFS support required for Hadoop workloads.

Azure Table storage (Option D): It is a NoSQL data store, but it is not designed for Hadoop Distributed File System support.

Therefore, for HDFS support in the context of migrating an on-premises storage solution to Azure, the appropriate choice is Azure Data Lake Storage Gen2 (Option A).

Azure Data Lake Storage Gen2: This is a fully managed, cloud-native data lake that supports the HDFS protocol. It allows you to store and analyze large amounts of data in its native format, without the need to move or transform the data.

https://learn.microsoft.com/en-us/azure/storage/blobs/data-lake-storage-introduction#key-features-of-data-lake-storage-gen2

Hadoop compatible access: Data Lake Storage Gen2 allows you to manage and access data just as you would with a Hadoop Distributed File System (HDFS). The new ABFS driver (used to access data) is available within all Apache Hadoop environments. These environments include Azure HDInsight, Azure Databricks, and Azure Synapse Analytics.

https://learn.microsoft.com/en-us/azure/architecture/guide/hadoop/apache-hdfs-migration

29) 1) a, 2) b

1 - Image storage:

a. Azure Blob Storage

Azure Blob Storage is a suitable choice for storing digital images, as it supports encryption at rest, handles large file sizes (up to 50 MB or even larger), and can be used in conjunction with Azure Web Application Firewall (WAF) on Azure Front Door.

The requirement to be accessible through a WAF limit the options to the Blob storage.

2 - Customer accounts:

b. Azure Cosmos DB

Azure Cosmos DB is a highly scalable, globally distributed, multi-model database service that supports automatic scale-out, ensures high availability even in the event of a datacenter failure, and allows for reading and writing data from multiple Azure regions. This makes it an ideal choice for storing customer account data in your scenario.

Reference:

https://learn.microsoft.com/en-us/azure/frontdoor/scenario-storage-blobs

https://learn.microsoft.com/en-us/azure/cosmos-db/introduction#guaranteed-speed-at-any-scale

30) A

A. Azure Cosmos DB for NoSQL

Azure Cosmos DB is a globally distributed, multi-model database service that supports SQL commands, multi-master writes, and guarantees low latency read operations. It supports a variety of NoSQL data models including document, key-value, graph, and column-family. Azure Cosmos DB provides automatic and instant scalability, high availability, and low latency globally by replicating and synchronizing data across multiple Azure regions.

On the other hand, Azure SQL Database and Azure SQL Database Hyperscale are traditional relational database services that do not natively support multi-master writes.

https://learn.microsoft.com/en-us/azure/cosmos-db/introduction#key-benefits

- Gain unparalleled SLA-backed speed and throughput, fast global access, and instant elasticity. Real-time access with fast read and write latencies globally, and throughput and consistency all backed by SLAs

- Multi-region writes and data distribution to any Azure region with just a button.

31) B

B. General Purpose

The General-Purpose compute tier provides a balance between performance and cost. It is suitable for most common workloads and offers a good combination of CPU and memory resources. It provides high availability and fault tolerance by utilizing Azure's infrastructure across multiple datacenters. This ensures that the databases remain accessible even if a datacenter fails.

The Burstable compute tier (option A) is designed for workloads with variable or unpredictable usage patterns. It provides burstable CPU performance but may not be the optimal choice for ensuring availability during a datacenter failure.

The Memory Optimized compute tier (option C) is designed for memory-intensive workloads that require high memory capacity. While it provides excellent performance for memory-bound workloads, it may not be necessary for minimizing costs or meeting the specified requirements.

https://learn.microsoft.com/en-us/azure/mysql/flexible-server/concepts-high-availability#limitations

Here are some considerations to keep in mind when you use high availability:

- High availability isn't supported in the burstable compute tier.

Extra explanation:

General Purpose (Option B): This compute tier is designed for a balance of performance and cost-effectiveness. It can provide good performance for a variety of workloads while keeping costs lower compared to the Memory Optimized tier. It's a suitable choice for scenarios where there is a need for a cost-effective solution without compromising on performance.

Options A (Burstable) and C (Memory Optimized) might not be the optimal choices in this scenario:

Burstable (Option A): This tier is designed for workloads with burstable performance requirements. It may not be the best fit for scenarios requiring high availability and accessibility in the event of a datacenter failure.

Memory Optimized (Option C): While this tier offers high memory and compute power, it might be more expensive than necessary for the given requirements, and the benefits of a memory-optimized configuration might not be fully utilized.

Therefore, for the specified requirements, the General-Purpose compute tier (Option B) is the recommended choice.

32) B

To fulfill the specified requirements of supporting SQL queries, supporting geo-replication, and enabling storage and access of data relationally in an application using Azure Cosmos DB, the recommended API is:

B. PostgreSQL

Explanation:

PostgreSQL (Option B): The Cosmos DB's API for PostgreSQL enables the use of PostgreSQL wire protocol, allowing applications using PostgreSQL to interact with Cosmos DB. It supports SQL queries and provides geo-replication capabilities. Additionally, it allows for storage and access of data relationally, making it suitable for applications with relational data models.

Options A (Apache Cassandra), C (MongoDB), and D (NoSQL) represent different APIs for Cosmos DB, but they may not fully align with the requirement for relational storage and access or support SQL queries in the same way as the PostgreSQL API.

Therefore, for the specified requirements, the recommended API is Cosmos DB's API for PostgreSQL (Option B).

https://learn.microsoft.com/en-us/azure/cosmos-db/choose-api

Store data relationally:

- NoSQL stores data in document format

- MongoDB stores data in a document structure (BSON format)

Support SQL Queries:

- Apache Cassandra uses Cassandra Query Language (CQL)

If you're looking for a managed open-source relational database with high performance and geo-replication, Azure Cosmos DB for PostgreSQL is the recommended choice.

33) 1) a, 2) b

1. Storage Type:

a. Azure Data Lake Storage Gen2

Azure Event Hubs Capture allows captured data to be written either to Azure Blob Storage or Azure Data Lake Storage Gen2. Given the nature of the data and its use in reporting and analysis, Azure Data Lake Storage Gen2 is the more appropriate choice because it is designed for big data analytics.

2. Data format:

b. Avro

Event Hubs Capture uses Avro format for the data it captures. Avro is a row-oriented format that is suitable for various data types, it's compact, fast, binary, and enables efficient and fast serialization of data. This makes it a good choice for Event Hubs Capture.

Reference:

https://learn.microsoft.com/en-us/azure/event-hubs/event-hubs-capture-overview#how-event-hubs-capture-works

Also:

The destination storage (Azure Storage or Azure Data Lake Storage) account must be in the same subscription as the event hub.

Event Hubs doesn't support capturing events in a premium storage account.

34) C

C. Azure Synapse Link for Azure Cosmos DB.

Azure Synapse Link for Azure Cosmos DB creates a tight integration between Azure Cosmos DB and Azure Synapse Analytics, allowing you to run near real-time analytics over operational data in Azure Cosmos DB. It creates a "no-ETL" (Extract, Transform, Load) environment that allows you to analyze data directly without affecting the performance of the transactional workload, which is exactly what is required in this scenario.

A. Azure Data Factory with Azure Cosmos DB and Azure Synapse Analytics connectors would require ETL operations which might impact the performance of the operational data store.

B. Azure Synapse Analytics with PolyBase data loading is more appropriate for loading data from external data sources such as Azure Blob Storage or Azure Data Lake Storage.

D. Azure Cosmos DB change feed doesn't directly address the need for analytics without affecting the performance of the operational data store.

Azure Synapse Link for Azure Cosmos DB is a cloud-native hybrid transactional and analytical processing (HTAP) capability that enables near real time analytics over operational data in Azure Cosmos DB. Azure Synapse Link creates a tight seamless integration between Azure Cosmos DB and Azure Synapse Analytics. It enables customers to run near real-time analytics over their operational data with full performance isolation from their transactional workloads and without an ETL pipeline

Reference:

https://learn.microsoft.com/en-us/azure/cosmos-db/synapse-link

35) 1) c, 2) a

Dynamic data masking helps prevent unauthorized access to sensitive data by enabling customers to designate how much of the sensitive data to reveal with minimal effect on the application layer.

https://learn.microsoft.com/en-us/azure/azure-sql/database/dynamic-data-masking-overview

Always Encrypted is a feature designed to protect sensitive data, such as credit card numbers or national/regional identification numbers (for example, U.S. social security numbers), stored in Azure SQL Database, Azure SQL Managed Instance, and SQL Server databases.

https://learn.microsoft.com/en-us/sql/relational-databases/security/encryption/always-encrypted-database-engine

DDM won't address the SSN requirement: "Administrative users and roles can always view unmasked data via the CONTROL permission, which includes both the ALTER ANY MASK and UNMASK permission. Administrative users or roles such as sysadmin, serveradmin, or db_owner have CONTROL permissions on the database by design, and can view unmasked data."

Reference:

https://learn.microsoft.com/en-us/sql/relational-databases/security/dynamic-data-masking?view=sql-server-ver16#permissions

36) B

In terms of supporting immutable storage, both Azure Data Lake storage and Azure Blob storage are correct. But ACL is supported by Azure Data Lake storage, not supported by Azure Blob storage.

Azure Data Lake Storage.

"Azure Data Lake Storage Gen2 implements an access control model that supports both Azure role-based access control (Azure RBAC) and POSIX-like access control lists (ACLs)."

https://learn.microsoft.com/en-us/azure/storage/blobs/data-lake-storage-access-control

"Immutable storage for Azure Data Lake Storage is now generally available."

https://azure.microsoft.com/en-us/updates/immutable-storage-for-azure-data-lake-storage-is-now-generally-available/

https://learn.microsoft.com/en-us/azure/data-lake-store/data-lake-store-comparison-with-blob-storage

37) 1) a, 2) a

Data Explorer + KQL

The scenario criteria map directly to Data Explorer "Decision Criteria" & tree in this link: When to use Data Explorer https://learn.microsoft.com/en-us/training/modules/intro-to-azure-data-explorer/4-when-to-use-azure-data-explorer

The scenario does not include anything that prevents the use of DE based on that link & Data Explorer CAN scale to PB (it's a big data platform)

The scenario doesn't specifically say "real-time" or say what's producing the data, but ingesting/storing PBs of data + interactive analytics ... to me that means "streaming + real-time analytics".

And KQL (Kusto Query Language) because that's the query language for Data Explorer.

Azure Data Explorer provides interactive analytics. It allows you to examine structured, semi-structured, and unstructured data with improvised, interactive, fast queries4. You can use Azure Data Explorer Web UI, web client for Azure Data Explorer, or Kusto.Explorer, a rich windows client for Azure Data Explorer. To connect to your Azure Data Explorer cluster, you can use Jupyter notebooks, Spark connector, any TDS-compliant SQL client, and JDBC and ODBC connections.

38) 1) a, 2) c

"Serverless is a compute tier for single databases in Azure SQL Database that automatically scales compute based on workload demand and bills for the amount of compute used per second. The serverless compute tier is available in the General Purpose service tier and currently in preview in the Hyperscale service tier."

Reference:

https://learn.microsoft.com/en-us/azure/azure-sql/database/serverless-tier-overview

39) 1) b, 2) d

1) Blob type:

b. Block

2) Enable:

d. The change feed

Explanation:

Blob type - Block:

Block blobs are suitable for point-in-time restore scenarios, especially when blob versioning is in use. Block blobs support the concept of versions, enabling you to maintain different versions of a blob over time.

Enable - The change feed:

The change feed is a feature that allows you to track changes to blobs in a storage account.

By enabling the change feed, you can capture and use the historical changes to implement point-in-time restore functionality.

Therefore, for point-in-time restore with blob versioning and blob soft delete, you should choose the block blob type and enable the change feed in the storage accounts.

Point-in-time restore for block blobs:

https://learn.microsoft.com/en-us/azure/storage/blobs/point-in-time-restore-overview

These mentions enabling the change feed:

https://learn.microsoft.com/en-us/azure/storage/blobs/point-in-time-restore-manage?tabs=portal#enable-and-configure-point-in-time-restore

40) 1) c, 2) b

Recommendation:

1) Upload and transform the data:

   c. Azure Synapse pipelines

2) Provide Restricted access:

   b. Azure Data Share

Explanation:

1) Upload and transform the data: ,

- Azure Synapse pipelines are suitable for orchestrating ETL (Extract, Transform, Load) workflows. They can be used to efficiently upload and transform research data from FabrikamVM1 to contosolake1, ensuring alignment with Contoso's data formats.

2) Provide Restricted access:

- Azure Data Share is designed for securely sharing data between organizations. It allows Contoso to share snapshots of the data in contosolake1 with Fabrikam, providing restricted access based on specific sharing agreements. This ensures that Fabrikam has controlled and limited access to the required data.

In summary, Azure Synapse pipelines for data upload and transformation, coupled with Azure Data Share for providing restricted access, would be an appropriate solution to meet the specified requirements.

For ETL operations use Azure Data Factory and Azure Synapse Pipelines are based on Azure Data Factory.

Source: https://learn.microsoft.com/en-us/azure/synapse-analytics/data-integration/concepts-data-factory-differences

For restricted access use Azure Data Share:

Azure Data Share enables organizations to securely share data with multiple customers and partners. Data providers are always in control of the data that they've shared and Azure Data Share makes it simple to manage and monitor what data was shared, when and by whom.

In this case snapshot-based sharing should be used.

Source:

https://learn.microsoft.com/en-us/azure/data-share/overview

41) 1) b, 2) a

1) To implement the data warehouse:

  b. An Azure Synapse Analytics dedicated SQL pool

2) To implement the serving layer:

  a. Azure Analysis Services

Explanation:

1) To implement the data warehouse:

  - An Azure Synapse Analytics dedicated SQL pool is designed for large-scale data warehousing. It supports the efficient loading of transformed data and provides a dedicated resource for analytics queries, making it suitable for handling large amounts of data from multiple sources.

2) To implement the serving layer:

  - Azure Analysis Services is a fully managed platform-as-a-service (PaaS) that enables the creation of OLAP models. It allows you to build semantic models for end-user consumption and provides a managed serving layer. With thousands of end users needing access, Azure Analysis Services is a scalable and efficient solution.

In summary, using an Azure Synapse Analytics dedicated SQL pool for the data warehouse and Azure Analysis Services for the serving layer would be appropriate for the specified requirements.

Data Warehouse: Azure Synapse Analytics (formerly SQL Data Warehouse)

Azure Synapse Analytics is a massively parallel processing (MPP) data warehouse that can handle large amounts of data and provides a scalable solution for analytics.

Managed Serving Layer: Azure Analysis Services

Azure Analysis Services provides a fully managed platform-as-a-service (PaaS) solution for online analytical processing (OLAP) and data modeling. It is suitable for serving analytical models to thousands of end users.

Here's how the pipeline would work:

Periodically export database updates to Azure Blob storage.

Use Azure Data Factory to cleanse and transform the data from Blob storage.

Load the transformed data into your Azure Synapse Analytics data warehouse.

Use Azure Analysis Services to create and manage OLAP models based on the data in your data warehouse.

End users can connect to Azure Analysis Services to query and analyze the data.

42) 1) a, 2) b

1) Service:

a. A single Azure SQL database

Selecting a single Azure SQL database means you are opting for an individual, standalone database. While this doesn't inherently provide multiple read-only replicas, it's worth noting that you can still configure read replicas manually using features like Geo-Replication or Active Geo-Replication. However, this might require more manual configuration and management effort.

2) Service tier:

b. Hyperscale

Hyperscale is a service tier within Azure SQL Database that provides automatic and dynamic scaling, including the ability to add read-only replicas. With Hyperscale, read-only replicas can be dynamically added or removed to handle varying workloads, and read-only requests are automatically load-balanced across these replicas. This aligns with the requirement for supporting multiple read-only replicas and automatically load balancing read-only requests.

In summary, while a single Azure SQL database can be configured with read replicas, the Hyperscale service tier provides a more automated and scalable solution with dynamic scaling and load balancing, which is beneficial for meeting the specified requirements.

43) B

B. Blob snapshots

Explanation:

To meet the requirements of restoring the last uploaded version of File1.txt from any day within a 30-day timeframe after the file was overwritten and minimizing storage space, you should incorporate blob snapshots. Blob snapshots are read-only versions of a blob that capture the state of the blob at a specific point in time. They provide a cost-effective way to maintain historical versions of a blob without duplicating the entire data set.

Explanation of options:

A. Container soft delete: This feature is not directly related to maintaining historical versions of individual blobs. It is used for recovering deleted containers within a specified retention period.

B. Blob snapshots: Blob snapshots allow you to capture the state of a blob at a specific point in time, providing a cost-effective way to maintain historical versions of the blob.

C. Blob soft delete: Blob soft delete is a feature that allows you to recover a deleted blob within a specified retention period. However, it may not be the most efficient way to maintain historical versions for a specific use case like this.

D. Blob versioning: Azure Blob Storage does not have a native versioning feature. However, you can achieve similar functionality using blob snapshots or implementing your versioning logic in the application.

In summary, using blob snapshots is the most appropriate option for meeting the specified requirements while minimizing storage space.

44) A

A. Azure Data Factory

Explanation:

Azure Data Factory is a cloud-based ETL service in Azure that is well-suited for automating the extraction, transformation, and loading (ETL) processes. It allows you to create data-driven workflows for orchestrating and automating data movement and data transformation. Given the requirement to seamlessly copy new data from on-premises data sources to Azure Data Lake Storage while minimizing administrative effort, Azure Data Factory is an appropriate choice.

Explanation of options:

A. Azure Data Factory: This is a cloud-based ETL service that enables data workflows for efficient data movement and transformation.

B. Azure Data Explorer: Azure Data Explorer is more focused on real-time analytics and interactive exploration of large datasets. While powerful, it may not be the best fit for a traditional ETL scenario.

C. Azure Data Share: Azure Data Share is primarily designed for sharing data between organizations or departments securely. It may not be the optimal choice for ETL processes.

D. Azure Data Studio: Azure Data Studio is a cross-platform database tool, more suitable for database development, querying, and administration, rather than for ETL processes.

In summary, Azure Data Factory (option A) aligns with the requirements of automating ETL processes and minimizing administrative effort for copying data to Azure Data Lake Storage.

So, Azure Data Factory is correct.

Big data requires a service that can orchestrate and operationalize processes to refine these enormous stores of raw data into actionable business insights. Azure Data Factory is a managed cloud service that's built for these complex hybrid extract-transform-load (ETL), extract-load-transform (ELT), and data integration projects.

Reference:

https://learn.microsoft.com/en-us/azure/data-factory/introduction

45) C

C. An Always On availability group

Explanation:

An Always On availability group is a feature in SQL Server that provides high availability and disaster recovery solutions. It aligns well with the specified requirements:

A. Azure virtual machine availability sets: While availability sets provide high availability within a datacenter, they are not designed for disaster recovery across regions.

B. Azure Disk Backup: This option doesn't inherently provide the ability to recover in the event of a regional outage, and it may not meet the specified RTO and RPO requirements.

C. An Always On availability group: This feature supports high availability and disaster recovery. By configuring an Always On availability group, you can ensure the ability to recover from a regional outage, achieve a low RTO (Recovery Time Objective), meet the RPO (Recovery Point Objective), and support automated recovery.

D. Azure Site Recovery: While Azure Site Recovery is a comprehensive disaster recovery solution, it might introduce additional costs. Always On availability groups can be a cost-effective solution, depending on the specific requirements and budget constraints.

In summary, an Always On availability group is a suitable recommendation to fulfill the specified disaster recovery requirements while minimizing costs.

Reference:

https://docs.microsoft.com/en-us/azure/site-recovery/site-recovery-faq

46) 1) c, 2) b

1. 36 months

2. 1 day (backup daily)

The backups are taken daily, not hourly. Instant recovery refers to the backup snapshot being available straight away instead of having to go to the vault first. So, this has nothing to do with backup frequency

the "instant" refers to the restore operation: the snapshot is kept local as well as in the vault so during a restore it can be mounted straight away instead of having to be restored from the vault first.

Reference:

https://learn.microsoft.com/en-us/azure/backup/backup-instant-restore-capability#whats-new-in-this-feature

https://docs.microsoft.com/en-us/azure/backup/backup-azure-vm-backup-faq#what-s-the-minimum-rpo-and-rto-for-vm-backups-in-azure-backup

47) A

A. Yes. This solution meets the goal. By deploying two Azure virtual machines in two separate Azure regions, you provide redundancy if one of the regions fails. Azure Traffic Manager can be used to distribute traffic between the virtual machines in different regions, ensuring high availability.

Additionally, deploying Azure virtual machines allows you to have access to the full .NET Framework and grants administrators the ability to access the operating system to install custom application dependencies.

- Traffic manager is global I.e. multi region

- layer 7 traffic balancer option.

https://learn.microsoft.com/en-us/azure/traffic-manager/traffic-manager-overview

Azure Traffic Manager is a DNS-based traffic load balancer. This service allows you to distribute traffic to your public facing applications across the global Azure regions. Traffic Manager also provides your public endpoints with high availability and quick responsiveness.

48) B

B. No

While Azure Application Gateway is a powerful tool for handling application traffic at the application layer and can assist with routing, load balancing, and other functions, it operates within a single region. It doesn't automatically provide geo-redundancy across multiple Azure regions.

For redundancy across regions, Azure Traffic Manager or Azure Front Door would be more suitable. They operate at the DNS level and are designed to route traffic across different regions for high availability and failover purposes.

So, in this case, deploying two Azure virtual machines to two Azure regions and deploying an Azure Application Gateway would not fully meet the stated goals due to the lack of a regional failover strategy.

App gateway cannot span regions.

App Gateway will balance the traffic between VMs deployed in the same region. Create an Azure Traffic Manager profile instead.

Extra explanation:

While deploying two Azure virtual machines to two Azure regions addresses redundancy, and an Azure Application Gateway can provide load balancing and traffic routing, it does not explicitly address the requirement of granting administrators access to the operating system to install custom application dependencies.

The Azure Application Gateway is primarily designed for load balancing and application delivery, and it does not provide direct access to the underlying operating system of the virtual machines. To meet the requirement of granting administrators, access to the operating system, you may need to consider alternative solutions such as Azure Virtual Machines configured with custom security groups or Azure Virtual Machine Scale Sets.

Therefore, the proposed solution does not fully align with the specified goal.

49) 1) b, 2) b

1) Storage tier:

b. Premium

Premium: Premium file shares are backed by solid-state drives (SSDs) and provide consistent high performance and low latency, within single-digit milliseconds for most IO operations, for IO-intensive workloads.

Incorrect Answers:

∞ Hot: Hot file shares offer storage optimized for general purpose file sharing scenarios such as team shares. Hot file shares are offered on the standard storage hardware backed by HDDs.

∞ Transaction optimized: Transaction optimized file shares enable transaction heavy workloads that don't need the latency offered by premium file shares.

Transaction optimized file shares are offered on the standard storage hardware backed by hard disk drives (HDDs). Transaction optimized has historically been called "standard", however this refers to the storage media type rather than the tier itself (the hot and cool are also "standard" tiers, because they are on standard storage hardware).

2) Redundancy:

b. Zone-redundant storage (ZRS)

Premium Azure file shares only support LRS and ZRS.

Zone-redundant storage (ZRS): With ZRS, three copies of each file stored, however these copies are physically isolated in three distinct storage clusters in different Azure availability zones.

Explanation:

1) Storage tier: Premium

- The Premium storage tier is designed for high-performance workloads and provides low-latency access, making it suitable for transaction-intensive applications.

2) Redundancy: Zone-redundant storage (ZRS)

- Zone-redundant storage replicates your data across multiple availability zones within the same region. This provides resiliency and high availability. In the context of minimizing latency and ensuring high resiliency, Zone-redundant storage is a suitable choice.

By selecting the Premium storage tier and configuring Zone-redundant storage, you can achieve low-latency access and the highest level of resiliency for your file shares when accessed from on-premises applications with frequent transactions.

Reference:

https://docs.microsoft.com/en-us/azure/storage/files/storage-files-planning#storage-tiers

50) B

A virtual machine scale set with autoscaling can meet the requirement of providing access to the full .NET framework and granting administrators access to the operating system to install custom application dependencies. However, it may not be the best solution for providing redundancy if an Azure region fails.

To provide redundancy if an Azure region fails, it is recommended to deploy the stateless web app across multiple regions using Azure App Service. Azure App Service provides built-in redundancy and failover support across regions. Additionally, Azure App Service can also provide access to the full .NET framework and grant administrators access to the operating system.

Therefore, the recommended solution would be to deploy the stateless web app using Azure App Service to provide redundancy and meet all the specified requirements.

Instead, you should deploy two Azure virtual machines to two Azure regions, and you create a Traffic Manager profile.

Note: Azure Traffic Manager is a DNS-based traffic load balancer that enables you to distribute traffic optimally to services across global Azure regions, while providing high availability and responsiveness.

Reference:

https://docs.microsoft.com/en-us/azure/traffic-manager/traffic-manager-overview

51) Answer area: 1) b, 2) a

1) Application1:

b. BlockBlobStorage with Premium performance and Zone-redundant storage (ZRS) replication.

Application2:

a. BlobStorage with Standard performance, Hot access tier, and Read-access geo-redundant storage (RA-GRS) replication.

Explanation:

- For Application1 requiring the highest transaction rates and lowest latency, using BlockBlobStorage with Premium performance ensures optimal performance. Additionally, Zone-redundant storage (ZRS) replication provides high availability in the event of a datacenter failure.

- For Application2 aiming for the lowest storage costs per GB, BlobStorage with Standard performance, Hot access tier, and Read-access geo-redundant storage (RA-GRS) replication is suitable. This configuration optimizes costs while still providing geographic redundancy.

Other options (c and d) either do not align with the specific requirements or may not be the most cost-effective or performance-optimized choices for the given scenarios.

52) 1) a, 2) a

Answer area:

1) Storage account type:

   a. Premium block blobs

2) Redundancy:

   a. Zone-redundant storage (ZRS)

Explanation:

1) Storage account type:

Premium block blobs

   - Premium block blobs offer high-performance storage and are suitable for scenarios where minimizing read latency is a priority. This aligns with the requirement to maximize data resiliency while minimizing read latency for business-critical data.

2) Redundancy:

Zone-redundant storage (ZRS)

- Zone-redundant storage replicates data across multiple availability zones, providing high resiliency. It ensures that the data remains available even in the event of a failure in one of the zones. This meets the requirement to maximize data resiliency for business-critical data.

Together, using Premium block blobs with Zone-redundant storage provides a storage solution that addresses the specified requirements for the new app.

To minimize read latency, premium block blobs is the right answer, the immutable storage is also supported on premium tier.

Reference:

https://docs.microsoft.com/en-us/azure/storage/blobs/immutable-storage-overview#supported-account-configurations

53) A

Front Door is an application delivery network that provides global load balancing and site acceleration service for web applications. It offers Layer 7 capabilities for your application like SSL offload, path-based routing, fast failover, caching, etc. to improve performance and high-availability of your applications.

Traffic Manager does not provide SSL Offloading.

And the other options are not global options (multi-region)

Reference:

https://docs.microsoft.com/en-us/azure/architecture/guide/technology-choices/load-balancing-overview

54) 1) c, 2) b

Recommended Options:

1) Storage Account Type:

c. Standard General-purpose v2

2) Redundancy:

b. Zone-redundant storage (ZRS)

Explanation:

Storage Account Type:

Standard General-purpose v2 (GPv2) is a versatile and cost-effective storage account type that supports storage tiers. It provides the flexibility to choose between hot, cool, and archive access tiers based on the access patterns of your data. Given the requirement to minimize costs and support storage tiers, Standard GPv2 is a suitable choice.

Redundancy:

Zone-redundant storage (ZRS) replicates data across multiple availability zones within the same region, ensuring availability if a single Azure datacenter fails. ZRS provides a good balance between redundancy and cost-effectiveness, aligning with the goal of minimizing costs while meeting the availability requirement.

Reference:

https://learn.microsoft.com/en-us/azure/storage/common/storage-redundancy#zone-redundant-storage

Zone-redundant storage (ZRS) replicates your storage account synchronously across three Azure availability zones in the primary region. Each availability zone is a separate physical location with independent power, cooling, and networking. ZRS offers durability for storage resources of at least 99.9999999999% (12 9's) over a given year.

With ZRS, your data is still accessible for both read and write operations even if a zone becomes unavailable. If a zone becomes unavailable, Azure undertakes networking updates, such as DNS repointing. These updates may affect your application if you access data before the updates have completed. When designing applications for ZRS, follow practices for transient fault handling, including implementing retry policies with exponential back-off.

55) 1) c, 2) d

In the rare event that an entire Azure region is unavailable, the requests that you make of Azure Key Vault in that region are automatically routed (failed over) to a secondary region except in the case of the Brazil South and Qatar Central region.

During failover, your key vault is in read-only mode. Requests that are supported in this mode are:

List certificates

- Get certificates
- List secrets
- Get secrets

- List keys
- Get (properties of) keys
- Encrypt
- Decrypt
- Wrap
- Unwrap
- Verify
- Sign
- Backup

Reference:

https://docs.microsoft.com/en-us/azure/key-vault/general/disaster-recovery-guidance

56) 1) c, 2) b, 3) a

1) c. Azure Site Recovery

Coordinates virtual-machine and physical-server replication, failover, and fullback.

DR solutions have low Recovery point objectives; DR copy can be behind by a few seconds/minutes.

DR needs only operational recovery data, which can take hours to a day. Using DR data for long-term retention is not recommended because of the fine-grained data capture.

Disaster recovery solutions have smaller Recovery time objectives because they are more in sync with the source.

Remote monitor the health of machines and create customizable recovery plans.

2) b. Azure Site Recovery and Azure Backup

Backup ensures that your data is safe and recoverable while

Site Recovery keeps your workloads available when/if an outage occurs.

3) a. Azure Backup only

Azure Backup

Backs up data on-premises and in the cloud

Have wide variability in their acceptable Recovery point objective. VM backups usually one day while database backups as low as 15 minutes.

Backup data is typically retained for 30 days or less. From a compliance view, data may need to be saved for years. Backup data is ideal for archiving in such instances.

Because of a larger Recovery point objective, the amount of data a backup solution needs to process is usually much higher, which leads to a longer Recovery time objective.

Reference:

https://lighthousemsp.com/whats-the-difference-between-azure-backup-and-azure-site-recovery/

Note: They put Finance and Reporting in reversed order in question, they may confuse people during exam.

57) B

Azure SQL Database Premium. It provides high availability and failover capabilities, including the ability to remain available in the event of a zone outage, and supports failover between replicas without any data loss. Additionally, it provides a good balance of availability and cost, making it the most cost-effective option among the choices that still meets the requirements for high availability and failover.

Zone-redundant configuration is not available in SQL Managed Instance. In SQL Database this feature is only available when the Gen5 hardware is selected.

To prevent Data Loss, Premium/Business Critical is required:

The primary node constantly pushes changes to the secondary nodes in order and ensures that the data is persisted to at least one secondary replica before committing each transaction. This process guarantees that if the primary node crashes for any reason, there is always a fully synchronized node to fail over to.

Reference:

https://docs.microsoft.com/en-us/azure/azure-sql/database/ high-availability-sla?view=azuresql&tabs=azure-powershell

58) B

App Service has not admin access to OS.

Linux apps in App Service run in their own containers. You have root access to the container but no access to the host operating system is allowed. Likewise, for apps running in Windows containers, you have administrative access to the container but no access to the host operating system.

While deploying a web app in an Isolated App Service plan provides access to the full .NET framework and grants administrators access to the operating system to install custom application dependencies, it does not inherently provide redundancy if an Azure region fails. To achieve redundancy, you would need to set up a multi-region deployment using Azure Traffic Manager or Azure Front Door, in addition to using the Isolated App Service plan.

Instead: You deploy two Azure virtual machines to two Azure regions, and you create an Azure Traffic Manager profile.

Note: Azure Traffic Manager is a DNS-based traffic load balancer that enables you to distribute traffic optimally to services across global Azure regions, while providing high availability and responsiveness.

Reference:

https://docs.microsoft.com/en-us/azure/traffic-manager/traffic-manager-overview

https://learn.microsoft.com/en-us/azure/app-service/operating-system-functionality

59) 1) a, 2) a

1) a. Azure SQL DB

2) a. Active geo-replication

Standard geo-replication no longer exists anyway

Reference:

https://learn.microsoft.com/en-us/previous-versions/azure/dn758204(v=azure.100)?redirectionfrom=MSDN

https://learn.microsoft.com/en-us/azure/azure-sql/database/features-comparison?view=azuresql#resource-limits

Azure SQL Database

-Read-only replicas

Read scale with 1-4 high availability replicas or 1-30 named replicas

0 - 4 geo-replicas

60) 1) a, 2) b

1) a. Adding a secondary replica to AG1

Reason:

Creating an Always On availability group on VM1 would not be necessary, as you already have an availability group (AG1) in place on your on-premises SQL Server instances.

By adding a secondary replica to AG1, you can provide a copy of DB1 that can be used for the migration. This will allow you to minimize downtime on DB1 by performing the migration on the secondary replica, while the primary replica remains available for use.

2) Perform the migration by using: b. Azure Migrate

Azure Migrate provides a simplified migration, modernization, and optimization service for Azure. All pre-migration steps such as discovery, assessments, and right-sizing of on-premises resources are included for infrastructure, data, and applications. Azure Migrate extensible framework allows for integration of third-party tools, thus expanding the scope of supported use-cases. It provides the following:

Assessment, migration, and modernization: In the Azure Migrate hub, you can assess, migrate, and modernize:

- Databases: Assess on-premises SQL Server instances and databases to migrate them to an SQL Server on an Azure VM or an Azure SQL Managed Instance or to an Azure SQL Database.

Reference:

https://learn.microsoft.com/en-us/azure/migrate/migrate-services-overview

Feel free to contact me on LinkedIn at "Georgio Daccache" for any assistance or questions. I'll be happy to help at any time.

GOOD LUCK!

www.ingramcontent.com/pod-product-compliance
Lightning Source LLC
LaVergne TN
LVHW051328050326
832903LV00031B/3418